For James
With Compliments
Susan 14-1-09

GW01471525

Touching The Heart of Milton Keynes

A Social Perspective

Susan Popoola

authorHOUSE®

AuthorHouse™ UK Ltd.
500 Avebury Boulevard
Central Milton Keynes, MK9 2BE
www.authorhouse.co.uk
Phone: 08001974150

First published by AuthorHouse 10/6/2008

ISBN: 978-1-4389-1763-4 (sc)

Printed in the United States of America
Bloomington, Indiana

This book is printed on acid-free paper.

DEDICATION

Dedicated to Mum and Eileen - I Honour You

Acknowledgements

To all the people of Milton Keynes who live here, work here and, over the years, helped to make it the special place that I call home. You inspire me.

I only began to gain a full picture of Milton Keynes and what it's really about through Common Purpose. Thank you, Kate, for inviting me to attend.

This would have never happened without the help of all the people who took the time to openly and honestly answer all my questions – even the most basic and stupid ones – or helped me in some other way. By this I refer especially to:

Michael Synott, Milton Keynes Discovery Centre; Steve Norrish and Rose Palmer, Milton Keynes Christian Foundation; Shaun Harriott, Milton Keynes College; George Ridley, LightForce International; Tom Bulman, Countec and Kate Bulman; Lyndsey Geddes, Emberton Dale; Kay Greenhalgh, CMK Partnership; Sheila Thornton, Milton Keynes Economic & Learning Partnership; Angela Rice, Community Mobiliser, Lakes Estate; Mike Costello, Rok; Tracey Peters, Woughton Parish Council; Myrian Metcalf, Community Artiste; Janette & Eammon Bobey, Netherfield Residents Association; Clarence Gill, Wolverton Resident; Jan Lloyd, Mayor of Milton Keynes; John Best, Former Chief Executive of Milton Keynes Council; Ruth Stone, MKVCO; Zena Flinn, Living Archive; Nnamdi Dime, Dimensional Solutions; and Keith Silverthorne at Crosslinks/Spotlight, the Lakes Estate.

For all those people who had encouraged me to make this dream a reality. Not much is achieved in life without the support of friends and family, so thank you all, most especially Sage who had such an amazingly ability to capture my vision. Also for Mindy, who guided me through the process of turning this dream into something special – without you it may have remained a dream.

For all the young people who took the time to speak to me and openly share their points of view with me – most especially the students of Milton Keynes College and Milton Keynes Christian Foundation. Although they were all happy for me to quote them in this book, I have not mentioned them by name for the simple reason that I believe it would be inappropriate to do so.

I would also like to thank all the staff at Starbucks, Kingston, Milton Keynes who were so friendly and polite on the numerous occasions I came to sit down with my laptop to work. I couldn't have asked for a better serviced office.

CONTENTS

A Bit About the Place Called Milton Keynes

Welcome to Milton Keynes!

Never be afraid to try something new.
Remember, amateurs built the ark,
Professionals built the Titanic.
Anon

Milton Keynes is synonymous with roundabouts and concrete cows. However if, after 40 years as a new town and centuries of prior existence (as a number of different small towns and villages), this was all that Milton Keynes had to offer, Milton Keynes would not be such a diverse place with people from all backgrounds, colours and creeds and an ever-growing population.

It would also not be deemed England's most successful new town and a showcase city visited by people from across the world who want to understand how to develop a successful new town, which is earmarked for growth into one of England's ten largest cities by 2030.[1]

I'm possibly not the most knowledgeable person on Milton Keynes as I've only been here for five years, but the more I learn about it, the more passionate and in love with it I become and the more I come to believe that there is a need for greater awareness of what Milton Keynes is really about for the people outside of the town, some of whom will never ever visit, but carry an often very strong opinion of the place. Of equal importance, I believe it is necessary for those of us who live and work in Milton Keynes to be more aware of the diversity it offers.

Recognising the limits of my experience and knowledge of Milton Keynes, I have taken the time to visit different parts and speak to different people who I know have a much clearer, in-depth knowledge than I do on specific areas.

---

[1] The seating in the theatre can be moved around to vary the capacity between 900 and 1400 people

Having done all of this, I am very conscious that I only just touch the tip of the iceberg as there is so much more that I have consciously or subconsciously omitted or am possibly unaware of. For this reason, I hope that what I have put together will inspire you to investigate and find out more. You can find a number of links on the Leverage Points website.[2]

As with everything in life there are negative things about Milton Keynes as well as the many positives. I have chosen to focus more on the positives: the possibilities and opportunities to overcome the negatives. I'm in no way deluded, but I don't believe it is constructive to focus on the things that have been tried that have not worked or the mistakes that have been made along the way, unless there is a direct lesson to be learnt from doing so.

It is therefore not a contradiction that on occasion I have been compelled to mention some of the 'mistakes' that have been made in order to explain some of the current circumstances and, I hope, to provide some suggestions on how to avoid them and to move forward into the ultimate future for Milton Keynes.

I also hope that, through this book, people outside of Milton Keynes will come to understand that while we love our roundabouts and concrete cows, there is so much more to be said of this vibrant town.

Fireworks and Birthday Cake

Let us celebrate the occasion
WITH WINE AND SWEET WORDS.
PLAUTUS

I didn't realise how much I'd come to appreciate Milton Keynes until its 40th birthday. I was about to go out in the morning when I heard a few large bangs. This brought a slow, big grin to my face as I remembered that it was the 23rd January 2007 – our 40th birthday. Yes indeed: Milton Keynes brings with it a sense of both belonging and responsibility. I went off to London for the day, excited and eager to get back home for the birthday celebration concert in the evening.

Prior to this, I hadn't really thought much of Milton Keynes being 40, let alone recognised the event was taking place, until I saw the concert advertised in the papers. In fact I didn't really know what to expect from the concert, but £5 for a concert ticket wasn't asking much so a couple of friends and I thought – why not? Let's do it.

It was a great concert, with a variety of music ranging from rock to pop to a disco inferno musical journey through time. There was something for everyone. One of the other great things about the concert was that all the artistes were either based in or originated from Milton Keynes. The atmosphere was absolutely electric and I received an additional charge from all the people I bumped into that I knew either personally or through my work, or knew of because of the positions they held within Milton Keynes such as Isobel McColl, the Council leader and the Council's former chief executive, John Best. There were also a number of schoolchildren who had stayed up late to join in the celebrations. Virtually everyone seemed to be there.

But at the back of my mind there was a concern. I couldn't immediately understand what it was, but later, when I went through the events of the day, I realised that there were some people missing.

There is a group of people in Milton Keynes (like the rest of England) that we often forget and hardly talk about unless something goes wrong. These are the people from the less prosperous areas of the town – sadly they seemed to be missing from the celebrations. I think I found it particularly saddening because these were of the earlier arrivals in Milton Keynes – they formed the foundation for the town we have today. Without them, the story of Milton Keynes may have been very different

With this in mind, I was very much looking forward to the Party in Park and all the other celebrations taking place in June. My hope was that with the variety advertised there would be something for everyone.

The events were planned so that there was something for everyone. It did, however, require business sponsorship to enable them to be free and accessible for everyone but, sadly, there was not as high a take-up as one would have hoped. It was however a lot of fun and a setup that I believe helped people who may have previously been marginalised to engage in the events and not be left out. It was a success and I do hope that it becomes an annual event.

The fact that the June events were more all-involving gives me some hope that all the people of Milton Keynes will be considered and involved in the future developments and changes that take place as it goes forward. This is because Milton Keynes is continually developing and changing, just as it has been doing for the last 40 years. There's always something new happening and, possibly, that's an indication of why the people who live here are so passionate about it.

The Enigma of the Cows

It is completely unimportant.
That is why it is so interesting!
Agatha Christie

With all the talk about concrete cows, you would think that they are all over Milton Keynes. The truth is that until recently, when the original cows were placed in the City Centre shopping centre, the only time I saw the concrete cows was on the odd occasion when I drove past a field in Bancroft, where there are some replicas of the original cows. I must add that to actually see the cows while driving you do have to drive very carefully as their presence is so obscure that it would be very easy to have an accident while straining to see them. Milton Keynes Dons mascots are two cows named Donnie and Mooie. To the best of my knowledge this just about sums up the presence of the cows in Milton Keynes. This, therefore, made me wonder for a long time why there is so much talk about them.

The cows don't even have an "amazing" history that makes them stand out as unique. The presence of the concrete cows date back to 1978 when they were made by a resident Canadian artist named Liz Leyh (with the aid of some students) as a leaving gift on her return to North America.

I believe the most significant thing about the cows is the experiences – or maybe I should say trials – they have faced over the years.

People outside of Milton Keynes are probably unaware that the cows have faced a number of "adventures", including a kidnapping of a cow by pupils for a ransom; being painted as zebras; and being beheaded, to mention a few very sad incidents.

Although none of the other Milton Keynes projects of the time, such as the Tin Man and Mushrooms at Beanhill and the Griffin on Eaglestone, can compete with the concrete cows for adventures, Milton Keynes has had a number of art projects over time. Indeed Central Milton Keynes has a fair amount of beautiful sculpture, and some more beautiful artwork is planned for the new football stadium.

As such, while the concrete cows do in many ways have a lot of significance within Milton Keynes, the manner in which Britons associate Milton Keynes with concrete cows remains an enigma to me.

ROUNDABOUTS

Roundabout 40
And still in love
MILTON KEYNES 40TH BIRTHDAY LOGO

When I moved to Milton Keynes from London, I found that whenever I told people where I had moved they would give me funny looks that are difficult to describe and, to demonstrate their vast knowledge of Milton Keynes, if they didn't mention the concrete cows, they would most definitely mention the roundabouts. What struck me with surprise about this was how negative most people are about the roundabouts. "There are too many roundabouts!" they would exclaim in exasperation. "I always get lost!" they would cry with frustration.

This has always elicited a passionate response from me as I try to explain that the roundabouts are a good thing as they form part of the grid system that make it easy for people to get from one part of Milton Keynes to another within a very short period of time and without the hindrance of traffic lights all over the place – even where there is no traffic. Many people will say that they can very easily get from one end of Milton Keynes to another within the space of 10, maximum 15 minutes – whilst keeping within speed limits. (The national speed limits apply to most of the main roads in Milton Keynes.)

This means that for people like me who very easily get lost, half an hour is always more than adequate to get where I'm going within Milton Keynes as even if I per chance miss my way I can very easily turn at the next roundabout to get back on track. This is very much unlike a place like London where (with all due respect) once you miss a turn, you get caught in traffic-congested one-way systems that may lead you to lose a lot of time.

So whilst people outside of Milton Keynes may laugh about our roundabouts, for the people who live here or understand the structure the roundabouts are something that we love and appreciate. One of the key things that helps to make Milton Keynes unique. As Milton Keynes continues to develop and grow, this is a key feature that I hope that we do not lose.

Forty, Four Hundred or Four Thousand Years?

*There is nothing new
except what has been forgotten.*
Marie Antoinette

I mention the continued development and growth of Milton Keynes as, while it has grown rapidly over the last 40 years since it was designated a new town on the 23rd January 1967, there are major plans for its continued development. It is and has been a great success. In fact it is seen as the most successful of all the 21 new towns designated between 1946 and 1970.

This is evident by the fact that it is now seen as a showcase town, with town planners from all over the world visiting the Discovery Centre to gain a clear understanding of urbanisation and how to successfully develop a modern city.

The fact that Milton Keynes was designated a new town in 1967 conjures up the impression that nothing existed in the area before then. The truth, however, is that the area now known as Milton Keynes has a very rich history, being populated even before the Roman era. Even when you focus on more modern times before the designation of Milton Keynes as a new City. On the outskirts of present-day urban Milton Keynes were a number of key towns which are Bletchley, Wolverton, Stony Stratford and Newport Pagnell and, further afield, Olney.

The importance of these towns in history cannot be understated. Bletchley is the home of Bletchley Park, where German and other Axis Countries' codes were deciphered. This aided the Allied forces' efforts in bringing the Second World War to an end. Olney is the place where John Newton wrote one hymn a week inclusive of the poignant and historical hymn, *Amazing Grace*. On a lighter note, the phrase "cock and bull tale" is said to originate from Stony Stratford. It is believed that coaches between London and Birmingham changed horses in the town at two of the main coaching inns – The Cock and The Bull. Squabbles between rival travellers from the two towns are said to have led to exaggerated stories. Stony Stratford no longer has The Cock and Bull inns, but it is now home to both The Cock and The Bull hotels.

Most importantly, as discussed later, a number of the people living in Milton Keynes prior to 1967 still live there today – a fact that is rarely mentioned.

Beyond the Enigma

Without mysteries, life would be very dull indeed.
What would be left to strive for if everything were known?
CHARLES DE LINT

Talking about the history of Milton Keynes brings me to what can be referred to as another myth. People generally believe that Milton Keynes is just a town based around a grid system – i.e. the roundabouts. This may be true of the newer, central parts. Most of the areas that existed prior to 1967 are, however, little towns in their own right just outside of the new town already mentioned. These towns, together with the gridded area, make up only 30% of Milton Keynes. Outside of the town there is a vast rural, or should I say, country, area, which makes up the rest of Milton Keynes. Although I had intended to explore all these areas when I first moved here, I am yet to do so, so although I'm aware that there is a vast richness within these areas with numerous stories of their own to be told, I intend to focus on the urban parts.

This takes us back to the grid system. Outside of Milton Keynes most people seem to be unaware that the much-mocked roundabouts form the basis of a grid system that enables people to rapidly move from one part of the city to the next.

For me it also means that it is difficult to get lost in Milton Keynes as the roads are marked with H's and V's: Horizontal and Vertical roads. It's why, when my friends from London laugh about the roundabouts, I always passionately explain the grid system and tell people that all you need to do is follow your H's and V's.

At the centre of the grid system is Central Milton Keynes – otherwise referred to as The Centre. While there is a growing residential element to The Centre, it is very much the commercial centre of the town. It houses big businesses such as Argos Head Office, Volkswagen Group UK Ltd, Coca cola Enterprise Ltd and Abbey, down to medium-sized businesses and a multiplicity of small businesses. In total there are almost 10,000 businesses across the City[3]. It is also the retail centre of Milton Keynes – home to two major adjoining shopping centres – Midsummer Place and the mile-long Centre MK. In response to the question of what shops can be found in the shopping centre, the answer almost has to be "What shops can not be found in the Centre?"

The Centre also houses the Church of Christ the Cornerstone. Built in 1992, it is the UK's first ecumenical city centre church. It serves as the home church to Christians from the various denominations inclusive of Anglican. Baptist, Catholic, Methodist and United Reform. All these denominations are represented in the Church worship and ministry.

I cannot mention the Church of the Cornerstone without also mentioning the Peace Pagoda at Willen. Though not in the Centre, it is another first and a major religious symbol. Built in 1980 by monks and nuns of the Nipponzan Myohoji, it is the first Peace Pagoda to be built in the western hemisphere, and is understood to enshrine sacred relics of the Lord Buddha.

Outside of central Milton Keynes each square of the grid system encompasses a housing estate, industrial estate or combination of the two. There is a lot of greenery between the estates, with trees sheltering the houses from the main road.

This means that Milton Keynes is full of beautiful greenery, which is very well maintained by the Parks Trust. I have on many occasions gone walking and seen employees of the trust cleaning up the public areas or repairing property.

It is also home to a vast amount of wildlife, with woods and a number of parks.

Milton Keynes is also characterised by 13 lakes of varying sizes, each with its own unique features. The largest is Willen Lake, which is popular for watersports. Others include Caldecotte Lake, the Blue Lagoon at Bletchley, Furzton Lake, and the Tear Drop Lake.

I mention how easy it is to get from one area to the next. This is very true if you have a car. The grid system makes it a driver's paradise as you can so easily get from one end of the city to the other within 10 to 15 minutes. If you don't have a car it is a bit more complicated unless you cycle. There is a fair distance between locations. I used to go to a church which was a three-minute drive from my house, but about 20 minutes rapid walking. In a place like London where you have a good (though not always efficient) transport system it would be a non-issue but unfortunately, in Milton Keynes, if you don't have a car and you don't or can't cycle you are reliant on public transport or taxis.

Sadly, the greatest weakness of Milton Keynes is our public transport system within the City as all we have is buses that do not run regularly. These shortfalls became apparent to me when, shortly after I moved here, I faced the unfortunate situation of having my car break down. With the dread of car repair bills hanging over my head, I wanted a way of moving around as cheaply as possible. I was disappointed to find that the buses only ran every half hour and left me with a 15-minute walk to get home. So I ended up travelling about by car. This was not cheap and with my impending car repair bill left me very squeamish.

SPORTING GOOD FUN

"If you can't fly, run.
If you can't run, walk.
If you can't walk, crawl,
but by all means, keep moving..."
MARTIN LUTHER KING

Milton Keynes is synomonous with a number of sports activities in England, as sport plays a key role in the town.

Touching on this, in 2000, the National Badminton Offices were opened in Milton Keynes, making it the training centre for England's world-class squad. Milton Keynes is also home to the National Hockey Stadium which, until late 2007, was the home of the MK Dons football club.

Yes, the trophy-winning Dons, led by Paul Ince, described by a local newspaper as "the brightest young manager outside of the premier-ship."[4] In 2003, the Dons moved from London to Milton Keynes to join a number of other local football clubs such as Wolverton and Bletchley Town. The Dons spent the vast majority of the 2007/08 football season at the top of League Two and I'm pleased to say they have not been promoted to League One. To add to our pride and joy the Dons also won the Johnstone's Paint Trophy at Wembley this year – a match that over 35,000 people from Milton Keynes went to watch. That's demonstrative of one of the benefits of the central location of Milton Keynes: it is easy to commute to and from London and other major cities in the country. Having come from London to Milton Keynes, like so many residents, it's great to see how the Dons have rapidly become very much a part of Milton Keynes, with a number of locals having given up allegiance to alternative football teams in support of the team. The state-of-the-art new stadium is iconic and a bonus for football fans and I believe it helps to create the atmosphere that will ultimately spur the Dons on to greatness. We are also looking forward to hosting

Manchester United one day soon too! Yes, we have great dreams, and history shows that our dreams do come true.

Our sporting prowess does not stop there: golf is also very popular in Milton Keynes and there are around 10 golf courses in and around the town. We also have a basketball team – the MK Lions, Marshall Milton Keynes Athletics club, which has produced Craig Pickering, amongst others; the United Netball Club, with three teams; MK Tennis Club; an Ice Hockey team – MK Lightning; and a regular hockey team, a karate club, the city of Milton Keynes Swimming Club and a darts club, to mention a few of the other sports represented.

This just scrapes the surface; we've already hosted the All-England/All-Nations football matches in 2007 and we're looking forward to hosting many more great events. It's an absolute must that Milton Keynes plays a major role in the 2012 Olympics. The truth is, it is just yet to be defined.

AND IF YOU DON'T LIKE SPORTS

Fun is Good
DR SEUSS

If I talk about the activities available in Milton Keynes, I will only be touching the tip of the iceberg and I'll obviously be highlighting some of my favourite activities – amongst other things. There is always something to do in or around Milton Keynes to meet most people's tastes. In a place the size of London it's there staring you in the face all over the place – in Milton Keynes there is a greater need to keep your ears and eyes open or ask the question. However the opening of the Discover Milton Keynes Shop in the City will, hopefully, make it easier to find out more about what is going on.

Central Milton Keynes is home to Milton Keynes theatre district which has not only a 900-1400 seat theatre[1], but also an art gallery, together with a number of clubs, pubs and restaurants. The theatre district is as such one of the main hangouts for young people over the weekends.

Next to the theatre district is the Xscape building which is home to Europe's largest indoor "real snow" ski slope, an indoor rock-climbing wall, a multiplex cinema, and a number of shops and restaurants. Xscape is complemented by Willen Lake (in East Milton Keynes) which offers a number of water activities.

Newly arrived is the Hub which, as the name suggests, is a hub of modern apartments, offices, hotels, shops and restaurants. For anyone who does not want to go to the Centre for food or entertainment, there are numerous pubs across Milton Keynes to be discovered, both within the town and the environs where you can get a drink, a good meal and, sometimes, live music.

For music, aside from musicals at the theatre, there is also live music at the Stables, and jazz at the Encore and the Spice Lounge, plus Caribbean music at the Oak Tree. There is also a major concert venue called the Bowl which has hosted different artiste ranging from Robbie Williams to Michael Jackson to Bon Jovi to Green Day. In fact, it's interesting to note that young people across the country are increasingly getting to know Milton Keynes for the concerts at the Bowl.

Places such as the different parks, lakes, and woods all make Milton Keynes great for both walking and cycling. Oh and I can't help but mention the arts exhibitions of local artists which take place at venues such as Linford Wood.

Another key area of specific relevance to young people is the Point, a key meeting point for young people. Although the Point is not as significant now as it used to be, when it first opened it was home to England's first multiple-screen cinema and drew visitors from as far afield as the other side of Bedford.

Business

Only those who risk going as far as possibly
Find out how far they can go.
T. S. Eliot

As a self-employed professional when I decided to move from London to Milton Keynes, a motivating factor for me was the beauty of the environment and its planned structure. However the ultimate determining factor that brought me was the fact that I became aware that Milton Keynes is a place where business is embraced and thrives.

Milton Keynes is home to a number of well-known and large businesses such as Abbey, Volkswagen, Coca Cola and Right Move. There are also a number of medium-sized organisations and ones with regional offices in Milton Keynes such as Pennine, Autoliv and Schuco. I believe the number of large- and medium-sized organisations will continually grow as Milton Keynes grows and develops. What stands out most to me, though, is the vast number of small businesses. I understand that over 80% of the businesses in Milton Keynes have 20 employees or fewer.

The development of small businesses has led Milton Keynes to be referred to as an entrepreneurial city with a can-do attitude. There is a thriving small businesses community that has developed and grown in the area. With a thriving business presence in Milton Keynes, networking has flourished. People often laugh and say that business networking is such an integral part of business life in Milton Keynes that you could network for a living.

Indeed, in addition to the local Chamber of Commerce, Federation of Small Businesses and a regional branch of the Institute of Directors, there are over 40 different business networks meeting across the city, for breakfast, lunch and evening drinks or dinner. These range from special interest groups such as the Construction network and Women in Enterprise to more generalist networks such as Midsummers Breakfast Club, Milton Keynes Netwalking, BNI, and Business Breakfast in MK.

In March 2008 Milton Keynes was reported to be the fastest-growing employer. Business support for both new and established organisations is also available through organisations such as Business Link.

MELTING POT

It takes every kinda people
to make the world go round
ROBERT PALMER, EVERY KINDA PEOPLE

As you drive through gridded Milton Keynes you can't really see much of the houses, as they are largely obscured by the trees which encompass each grid square. It is therefore easy to understand why people may be deceived into thinking that each estate is pretty much the same as the next. The truth is that each estate has its own special, distinguishing features and variations which differentiate the developments on each of the new estates – even where the same developer has been at work.

It's a similar situation with the people. Outside of the centre and the outskirt towns, for the most part you hardly see the people walking about. Hidden behind the trees and at times within the houses are people from all walks of life. All ages, professions, nationalities and socio-economic backgrounds. It took me quite a bit of time to realise it but yes, Milton Keynes, like every other town or city in the country, represents people from all different socio-economic circumstances, including those who are economically deprived, who we so often forget.

Milton Keynes has as diverse a religious population as anywhere. It's home to Christians of various denominations, Hindus, Sunni and shi'ite Muslims from different national origins and Buddhists, to mention some of the main groups. Regardless of the differences, Milton Keynes has an interfaith group aimed at "encouraging dialogue and trust between the faith communities, and promoting a multi-faith presence in the civic and cultural affairs of Milton Keynes".5

Milton Keynes is also represented by the ever-growing diverse communities that are coming to be a part of England. The communities that I will, however, focus on are the more traditional English communities that I remember from when I was young – the neighbourhood communities where people support each other and look out for each other. Though they are not always immediately recognisable, they do exist in pockets – often in the least-expected areas consisting of both the traditional English population and people from all different backgrounds who live and work alongside them. These are paramount, because to me they represent the very heart of Milton Keynes. The heart that people so often say does not exist here.

Forever Changing – Growth

*"Even if you're on the right track
you'll get run over if you just sit there."*
Will Rogers

With a population of 227800 in 2007 and estimated growth of 12 people per week with a planned population of 320000 by 2030, the population of Milton Keynes is definitely on a continual rise.

From where I sit as an ex-Londoner, I can see many obvious reasons for the continued development and growth of Milton Keynes. While housing is not cheap, it is still much more affordable than places such as London. You also get much more land space. Milton Keynes is a very central location in England with good transport/travel networks which means that you can get from to London or Birmingham in around 40 minutes. It is about 30 minutes to Luton airport, from where you can now travel as far as New York or Dubai, and there are also some very good road networks connecting it with the rest of the country.

As I've mentioned previously, for me Milton Keynes is a self-sufficient town that has almost anything you want or need, with relatively more affordable housing. Simultaneously, it is close enough to London to visit and family and friends at the drop of a hat. I believe the same would apply to anyone moving to Milton Keynes from places such as Birmingham, Oxford or Cambridge.

More pertinently, however, in addition to Milton Keynes' natural attraction as a place to live, there is the central government agenda pushing for increased housing in the south east and specifically the Thames Valley gateway. I believe that as Milton Keynes has been such a success as a new town, it has become victim to itself being targeted for rapid growth of almost 29% from its current size by 2030. This will bring the population to the same size as a city such as Bristol.

As this has come from central government, there is a view that we don't have much of a choice in the matter. In achieving this, as I guess we therefore must, a key challenge is to ensure that as we build houses for the ever-growing population, we ensure that we build and maintain the infrastructure to cope with the growth.

It is also important to ensure that as we develop Milton Keynes for newcomers, we think about all of them – both those who can afford to buy the more exclusive modern housing and those for whom housing that is more affordable should be available to either buy or rent.

It is also important to ensure that, while developing for the new-comers, we make sure that the current residents are not forgotten. That regeneration takes place to ensure that the older parts of Milton Keynes (both from the pre-new town era and the early days of the new town) are not left to degenerate. That when we do go to regenerate these areas we take account of what the local residents want and need.

But we need to think of the current residents of Milton Keynes, not only from the perspective of regeneration, but also the vision that we bought into that has made so many people proud to call it home. So as the local government and Milton Keynes work to develop Milton Keynes, I hope they take the time to take cognisance of the views of the people who may express contrary views for no other reason than the simple fact that they want the best for the town.

It seems that the Centre of Milton Keynes is being developed to reflect a cafeteria culture for professionals. This may be appropriate for the Centre. However, as we begin to plan the redevelopment of places such as Wolverton, we need to ensure that whatever we do reflects the needs of not only people who may move into an area, but also the current local residents. This may mean that a cafeteria environment may not be best suited to a place like Wolverton that has an older and family population.

NOT SURE ABOUT A CASINO, BUT ...

Dear Lord, help me break even
I need the money
ANON

Milton Keynes has been earmarked for a casino. While I'm not against people gambling if they want to, I don't remember any consultation taking place that led to a conclusion that the residents wanted a casino. I'm all in support of the development and growth of Milton Keynes. I also recognise that I won't like everything that is done. However, I simultaneously believe that we need to look at both sides of the coin when we think of embarking on major projects. The new football stadium is something that I believe the vast majority of people will view from a positive perspective. I, however, see the casino differently.

I must be honest. While I'm conscious that it is important for the needs of the different people to be met and I'm conscious of the fact that there are developers ready and willing to include a casino in their developments, I'm not keen on the idea and, of all the people that I've spoken to, I've hardly come across any who say they would love a casino in Milton Keynes.

This is said to be positive because it will lead to regeneration by creating new jobs. It does not, however, feel right to me and maybe I have watched too many movies, but I believe it has far-reaching negative implications. Aimed at increasing the diversity of activities, buildings and spaces of culture, leisure, residential and employment opportunities as casinos are seen to appeal to a diverse range of age groups, sexes and cultures. It is also aimed at helping to regenerate socially deprived areas of the city

This will be an experiment and, although Milton Keynes has a love for the new, this is something that I would prefer us not to be a test ground for as if it goes wrong the impact will be almost irreversible and it could, potentially, do more harm than good to the areas it is supposed to help.

All this is to say that Milton Keynes is a great place; if you look beyond the stories of roundabouts and concrete cows, it has always been something special. It can be seen as a little Los Angeles from the perspective that it is a place to come if are, or want to become, an entrepreneur. A place of growing beauty and charm, that truly has something for everyone. A place that I'm convinced can only get better as long as we take care to think carefully through all our actions and next steps without being over-pressurised by Government.

A Commuter City?

"Not everything that counts can be counted,
and not everything that can be counted counts."
ALBERT EINSTEIN

While Milton Keynes has a thriving business community, I believe the typical size of businesses means that there are a limited number of high-income, senior-level positions within the city. This also means that the jobs do not align with the cost of housing. While I think this will change over time as more and more larger organisations move to Milton Keynes, currently a consequence is that about 20,000 people living here commute to such places as London where there are more higher-income jobs. Simultaneously, around 24,000 of the workers in Milton Keynes come from neighbouring areas of Milton Keynes or further afield.

A key point to this is that a large number of the people who live in Milton Keynes don't actually work here, while a large number of people who work in Milton Keynes don't live here. Subsequently there are only so many people who both live and work here. Especially when you take account of the fact that a number of entrepreneurs will be based in Milton Keynes but not work in the town.

There are a number of reasons why this is of significance. 21st century living tends to dictate that we are constantly on the move – busy. The regular commuter is typically up and out by 6 or 7 in the morning and is lucky to get home by 7 or 8 in the evening. Tired! Especially if they have been faced with train problems for the 2nd or 3rd consecutive day, or got caught up with traffic on the motorway on the way home which has extended a normally long day by an additional hour or two. Here I have described the 9 to 5 worker as opposed to the one who works long hours, which is still not uncommon in spite of the rise in flexible working. The long-hours culture also means that even the worker who lives close to home does not always get home bright and early.

If my observations (which I must hasten to say are not statistically based) are accurate, the typical professional/entrepreneur is likely to fit into one of five family groups: the single professional, the professional couples without children, the couple with about two school-aged children, the couple with grown up children, and the single parent with children (as there are an increasing number of them). I don't believe my deductions are rocket science and with that confidence I will go on to say that a significant number of Milton Keynes professionals typically have school-aged children.

A large number of these people will have migrated from places such as London to get away from congestion, to find a more affordable cost of living, because of social issues, and for better schools for their children. One of the key consequences of this is that they often don't have an extended family network around.

This means that while there may be a limited amount of time spent at home with the family (due to working hours and the amount of time spent commuting) there is also an absence of extended families to augment their time, and little time to get to know the people within the neighbourhood and gain a wider appreciation for things going on outside of their natural circle. The leisure time that is available is therefore very much focused around family.

As such our focus is on our needs and what we believe has a direct impact on us and our needs. So, caught up in the rat race, we work to provide the best for our children and prepare for retirement, while we strive to satisfy our important material needs that give us a sense of purpose in between the two.

I believe it's safe to say that this scenario helps to explain why people such as me are often consciously or subconsciously largely unaware of the other people within a community unless we are made aware of them because things are going wrong.

FARMERS & RAILWAY WORKERS

A thousand different sorts of trees,
With their fruit were to be met with,
And of a wonderful delicious odor.
CHRISTOPHER COLUMBUS

In school we are taught that Christopher Columbus found America in 1492. This gives the impression that, prior to his arrival in the Americas, no one lived there. The truth, however, is that several hundred groups of Native Americans lived in America before his arrival.

Similarly there were people in the area of Milton Keynes prior to 1967. The designated area of Milton Keynes in fact consisted of three small towns and 13 villages. The Milton Keynes village was in fact the smallest all the 13 villages. The whole of the designated area had a population of approximately 40,000.[6]

It is therefore impractical to say that Milton Keynes started from nothing 40 years ago. It's important for us to acknowledge the people who were here before and to be mindful of them and their needs as we develop Milton Keynes going forward.

It is interesting to note that before the concept of Milton Keynes emerged that Bletchley was hoping to develop and expand into a major town within the area. With the plans for Milton Keynes this, however, failed to happen and as the focus has very much been on the development of new estates, it is only in recent years that real attention has been paid to the redevelopment of the old towns.

One of the things I've noticed is that in the future development there seems to be much more of a focus on the people we are trying to attract into Milton Keynes than the people already living here. In a similar way, I get the impression that over the last 40 years there has been little focus on the wants and needs of the original inhabitants. I believe this has gone on to transcend to the earlier arrivals to Milton Keynes.

I'm not in a position to mourn what was. I am, however, in a position to begin to understand a sense of loss. To feel that some people believe they have paid a heavy price for Milton Keynes and as a result to feel a sense of sadness that things worked that way. I do not however stop here, I go on to hope that regeneration will constitute something meaningful to the people of Wolverton, Stony and Bletchley, representing what they want as opposed to what other people believe they need.

And Then They Came from All Around

Home is where you can scratch
Where it itches

The earliest arrivals to the new City of Milton Keynes were the people who moved into the grid squares of settlements of places such as Netherfield, Beanhill and Coffee Hall. A lot of questions were asked about the development of these areas and why things were done in the way they were. These areas tend to house people of the description outlined earlier. Typically the people who reside in areas such as Netherfield and Beanhill are not professionals or entrepreneurs. They typically tend to be people at the lower income end of society. In fact in Beanhill, almost 50% of residents are unemployed. There are different reasons for this, which I will try and touch on later. An important point, however, is that while they are not the most vocal part of society, they are an important part of the community which is often hidden away and forgotten unless something goes wrong.

People who fit into these categories are not unique to Milton Keynes, but are present in almost every town or city across the country. As these are such new areas, it is important to understand how we have so rapidly developed areas with such pronounced economic deprivation.

However, Milton Keynes has attracted people from all over the country and beyond from all spheres of community. Over the years, as the population grows, there has also been an increasing number of babies born in Milton Keynes who grow up here and see the new town of Milton Keynes as their home town.

A Few Things on My Mind

THOSE WHO WERE BORN HERE

*A baby is born with a need to be loved
and never outgrows it.*
FRANK A. CLARK

According to Milton Keynes Intelligence Observatory[7], as of 2003 approximately 16% of the population is between the ages of 15 and 24, of which a significant proportion would have been born in Milton Keynes. I believe those numbers will now be much higher. Sadly a number of these young people are NEET i.e. Not in Employment, Education or Training. Furthermore, although I don't have figures for Milton Keynes, and while the government may dispute this, according to the Princes Trust we lose an estimated £10 million a day due to the productivity loss to the economy as a result of young people.[8] I have also heard people refer to the current generation of youth as "the lost generation".

This means that the lives of young people around us are important not only because they are human beings and our children, or due to the fact that they are designated to look after us when we are old, but for the more immediate fact that that we have a moral responsibility. If none of this causes you to pause and think, the economic cost that will be incurred if they are not effectively educated, trained and employed should – because if they are not in a position to support themselves, we will have to support them.

There is also the question of the next generation coming after this generation. Even if we believe the current generation is really lost, how do we ensure that we don't lose the next one if we don't learn from the mistakes of the past? We can't necessarily have an impact on all the young people in the world, but we can do something (or in many cases, something more) regarding the young people around us here in Milton Keynes (or wherever we are).

The first question that comes to my mind is: Have the young people really changed that much from when we were young? I mean are they fundamentally different from the way we were when we were growing up and if so, how and why? There is no disputing the fact that we now live in a technological age where young people have access to computers which can do all sorts of weird and wonderful things, Playstations, Xboxes, Wiis, iPods and all sorts of other computer games. It is also true to say that technology has brought about new forms of communication which mean that we can readily communicate with people all across the world and that we can readily access information on things going on in different parts of the world. It is understandable that young people today are more aware of technology and are much more able to use it then older people because they have grown up with it. This is definitely a fundamental shift as it is very much a part of their everyday life: the use of technology intertwined into the school curriculum and used as an aid to learning. Although people often complain about young people and the use of technology there is often a lot of positive that comes from its use.

However, if we put the use of technology and the means of communication aside, what has really and truly changed? As a starting point to begin to understand this, think back to when you were young and the things you used to do. Are they really that different from the things that the young people of today do? In some ways I'm sure that they are, but largely I think things are very much the same.

But let us cite some examples using people we know very well. I don't say this maliciously, but rather in order to highlight what the vast majority of us were like when we were young, including the most successful of us... Let's start with David Cameron. David is someone who is fortunate to have gone to Eton, one of the best schools in England. Like a number of people he went to school with, he is said to have messed around with drugs and done other mischievous things. While I don't actually agree with the use of drugs, the most important point is what he has become today - the leader of the Conservative party who has aspirations of becoming Prime Minister.

Let's look at the person who was, until recently, prime minister: Tony Blair. It's been reported that when he was in school he constantly questioned the authority of his teachers.[9] Eventually he matured beyond this and rose to become Prime Minister. George Bush was rumoured to be a bit of a drinker, but fortunately he's gone beyond that and is now President of United States of America. Maybe you'd say that these are far-fetched cases, but we've also got people such as Richard Branson, who only just managed to finish school and now runs a multi-million-pound business. I can also think of so many people I know personally who have succeeded in spite of the predictions that had been made about them.

I remember when I was in school, while I wasn't necessarily bad, I most definitely was not the best-behaved pupil - I did not always do what was right, I rebelled and at times pushed the boundaries as far as possible. While I do not condone bad behaviour I still wonder what is it that young people do today that is so different to what we did when we were young? I'm not trying to justify what is wrong. I am however questioning our response to them. I believe at times our responses to them are extreme and in fact we actually have a tendency to look down on them and judge them. We seem to take very little time to talk to them and understand where they're coming from.

Take the instance of the whole thing about gangs. As soon as we see a group of young people together we tend to condemn them as gangs. If we see a group of older people together we don't think of them as gangs! What is the difference between the two groups? The point is that while there are some youth gangs, not all young people who hang out together are gangs. Furthermore while there are gangs that are very bad and dangerous, most are really about hanging out with friends who they can identify with.

The perception of young people seems worsened when we see them wearing tops that have hoods. Especially if they have the hoods up. It is a fact that there are young people who go around committing crimes and use the hoods as a form of disguise. However, more often than not for the majority of young people a hood is a fashion statement. It's something that they wear possibly because people they want to emulate, who they see on television or elsewhere, wear them. It's something that they might wear to look cool, to help them to feel that they are part of a group or, in some cases, it might actually be as an act of rebellion against the people who tell them not to wear them because they don't like them.

The truth is there is really nothing wrong with a hood aside from the fact that some people have used them in criminal activities, which has led us to criminalise them. More often than not this simply leads young people to rebel and to wear them all the more. Young people today, just like young people when I was young, don't like being told what to do. They are much more inclined to respond when people take the time to talk to them and reason things through with them.

What we forget when we complain about hoods is that young people buy them because they're available to be bought in shops. If they weren't sold, nobody could buy them - young people and old people alike.

As I've said, young people hang around in groups referred to as gangs wearing hoods, which leads us to refer to them as criminals or at least to treat them as such when we see them across over the road; we refuse to talk to them or even acknowledge them. The question then is: What would we have them do? What is available for them? When I was young there were a number of youth clubs around, amongst other activities

These days the facilities available to young people seem to be somewhat limited. There are still youth clubs, though they don't seem to be as numerous as before. In Milton Keynes, because of the structure, they seem to be much more spread out and therefore difficult to get to, and the opening hours do not tend to meet the needs of young people.

If you're a young person from a family where your parents can readily take you around to the city centre or other places where there are activities going on, you are much better positioned to go to places where you can have fun. If, however, you do not have parents who can take you around you may have to rely on the buses. Unfortunately the buses in Milton Keynes are quite limited. There is also a cost to this: for young person, it's not a cheap way of getting around. One of the unique features of Milton Keynes for getting around are redways. Unfortunately, however, they are underutilised. I have heard that people don't believe that they are safe. It's a shame, and I'd love to see something done about this.

So where does this leave young people? Specifically those who do not have parents or adults who can take them around and do not feel able to bear the cost of buses. Local facilities are quite limited and where they do exist they seem to be generally underutilised and not always open at times at times when young people would want to use them.

What Are We All Looking For?

Many of us spend our lives searching for success
when it is usually so close
that we can reach out and touch it.
RUSSEL H. CONWELL

When are we talk about the different people of Milton Keynes – and for that matter people across the world – it is very easy to focus on the differences. The truth, however, is that in as much as we are all human there are more similarities between us than there are differences. I believe this becomes most apparent when we take the time to stop and think about the things that we all want and, even more pertinently, need.

Way back in the 1940s our needs were described by Abraham Maslow as the hierarchy of needs. Just in case you are unaware of the work of Maslow, he describes what we as human beings need as levels of need, which are often shown in a pyramid form. The four lower levels, described commonly as deficiency needs, from the lowest level upwards are our psychological needs such as the need to breathe, eat, drink and sleep, without which we cannot live. These are followed by our need for safety and security. Next comes our need to feel loved and to belong to something. Following on from here are our "esteem" needs: self-esteem, confidence, achievement and both the need to be respected and to be respected in return. The fifth and highest level is the need for self-actualisation, where there is a focus on morality, creativity, spontaneously, problem-solving, lack of prejudice and acceptance of blacks.

I believe the key differentiation between human beings arises at the degree to which our needs are met. For an individual whose basic needs are not fulfilled the person is highly unlikely to be focused on the higher self-actualisation needs that might be of paramount importance to an individual who has all his or her lower needs met. I think that it's important that, when we look at people and observe their behaviours, we become more aware of where they are in terms of their needs and what has or has not been met in order to understand why they behave the way they do. There are certainly needs that we tend to focus on a lot in today's society.

Predominately however we tend to focus on wants and needs from the perspective of what we want or need from other people, as opposed to what they may need from us or the world at large. When people do not respond as we expect them to or we do not get what we want, there is a tendency for us to demand what we want or expect, and to view others from a negative perspective.

I Need a Roof over my Head

I need a roof over my head,
I need a roof over my head,
And bread on my table,
And bread on my table.
MIGHTY DIAMONDS

The lyrics to this song started ringing in my head after a visit to Netherfield, when I heard about the problems with the roofing in some of the housing. I didn't know at the time who sang the song – I just had the lyrics in my head because they are representative of the needs I saw. As I said, they are very basic and are representative of some of our basic physiological and safety needs.

It is perhaps understandable that the majority of people believe that problems around the lack of basic needs are non-existent in the West, but are limited to the developing world. It is sad to say that this is, unfortunately, very far from the truth. The 2005 hurricanes in America washed out the truth in the States, highlighting areas of poverty. Poverty in America was once again highlighted by the American Idol programme, "Idol Gives Back"[10]. This highlighted the cases of people who could not read or write, people living on the poverty line and people still suffering from the aftermath of hurricane Katrina in New Orleans.

England is not without areas of economic deprivation and although we have a welfare system that was set up to help, I believe there are times when it would not be unfair to say that it actually perpetuates the problem, and the fact that it is still very heavily relied on tells its own story. There are areas of deprivation scattered all across the country and it's sad to say that Milton Keynes – specifically some of the earlier developed areas – has some of the highest levels of deprivation in the country.

The positive thing is that although there is a question in my mind as to how effective the efforts are, a lot is being done to counteract the problems. On the other hand there is a sad reality that some of the problems are things that should never really have been long-term issues, such as problems with the roofing of houses in Netherfield (which have been in existence for a very long time) and should have been resolved a long time ago. At a certain point in time, European funding was made available to resolve the problem with some of the roofs. Unfortunately, there are still a number of residents who are still living with poor-quality roofing.

The repair of these roofs is the type of thing that I believe would make a very distinct difference to the quality of life of the people living in such places. People from outside of such an area may at times get frustrated by the "limited" aspirations of residents, but I believe that while they are tied down by the want of fulfilment of basic needs such as good quality housing, for many, their self-esteem and confidence are likely to be limited and they are unlikely to be focused on self-actualisation.

One of the potential solutions to poor quality housing and deprivation that has been presented is to pull down houses and replace them with homes of a better quality. Possibly this is a solution; however, one of the biggest concerns that I have already had with this form of solution is that, regardless of the problems with the housing, these are people's homes. Some of these people have lived in these houses for close to 40 years, so is it really right to knock them down? I would hate for someone to come and knock my house down and tell me to move elsewhere, away from my family, friends and neighbours.

A knock-on effect of this approach is the issue of the increasing cost of housing. Let's take the hypothetical example of Fred. He bought his house 35 years ago for £40,000 and he has managed to pay off his mortgage. The house is now valued at £180,000. If his house is to be demolished, he will receive compensation, but I doubt if it would cover the current value of his home or be enough to enable him to buy a new home. He would be forced to either rent a home or buy a new home on a mortgage. The question, therefore, is: Will he be better or worse off? He will have been moved away from a neighbourhood where he had concerns with the quality of his housing, but he will be faced with the problem of a new mortgage (if he can actually afford one) in a completely new environment.

As it stands it is already a frustration for many that there is no housing available that is affordable for their children, when a key reason why they moved to Milton Keynes was based on the under-standing of a promise of homes both for them and their children.

COMMUNITIES AND SOCIETY

There is no class so pitiably wretched
as that which possesses money
and nothing else.
ANDREW CARNEGIE

I constantly hear (and at times join in) the reminiscing of people about life when they were young. One of the things that always seems to come up is the sense of community that existed, whereby people looked out for each other in a way that meant that you could leave your door unlocked and know that no one would break in; that, as a child, you knew that if you misbehaved someone would give you a right talking to and if you dared go home and complain, you'd only be asking for more trouble. Possibly to some extent we romanticise some of things that took place.

There is, however, no doubt in my mind that there were clear structures in place. They may have had cracks and faults, but they did work. For instance, there was the local policeman who knew the people within the community where he worked. If he saw someone doing something wrong, he was in a position to talk to them, and they respected his authority and responded. Policemen now don't generally know the people within their communities unless they are people who have been caught on the wrong side of the law. It seems that everything they do must follow formal procedures and the citizens they talk to seem to be very much aware of their rights, and very ready to exercise them. The police don't seem to be able to use their discretion as they used to, and people definitely do not give them the type of respect that they had in the past.

Another key structure that seems to have been changed is that of schools. When I was young, teachers were seen as figures of authority and were given huge amounts of respect. You could get into trouble for talking back to a teacher and, though I am not an advocate of the cane, teachers were in a position to administer discipline to pupils, be it the cane, lines or what have you. Furthermore, from all the conversations that I have with people, it was very rare for parents not to support the actions of the teachers.

As I mentioned earlier, these systems were not perfect; they had cracks and faults, but rather than repair the faults we seem to have torn the systems down and reduced their effectiveness. So now it is commonplace to hear that a teacher was threatened by a pupil and that the teacher had very limited powers to do anything about it.

This is heightened by the fact that as these structures have been torn down, they have not been replaced and at the same time people have been made very much conscious of our growing number of rights, without been informed of our equally important responsibilities.

So we reminisce over the times when there was a sense of community and people looked out for each other. I am of the impression that there are, however, places where people are still fighting to maintain a sense of community. Specifically when you talk to people in the areas that are isolated – imposed or otherwise – you will find that even if they are presented with an opportunity to leave and move elsewhere, a number of them will not want to do so, because regardless of their environment, there is a sense of community.

RESPECT

Where did we ever get the crazy idea that in order to make children
do better, first we have to make them feel worse?
Think of the last time you felt humiliated or treated unfairly.
Did you feel like cooperating or doing better?
JANE NELSON

The 21st century youth receive a lot of flak for their attitude and their lack of respect. So I ask the question: What is respect? A simple dictionary definition of respect is "to treat with consideration"[11] This is something that I believe everyone should apply to everyone else. The only problem is that a number of young people (that I've spoken to) don't believe that they are shown any respect by older people.

Take the example of Dan (not his real name). When I spoke to Dan he said he was actually tired of being disrespected by adults. He had concluded that the only way to defend himself against the disrespect that adults constantly showed to him was to show no respect to them. I don't agree with his response, but for his part, he couldn't understand why it was that he would hold the door open for an adult and there wouldn't be a word of thanks in return. Why he'd see a lady struggling with her shopping, offer to help and be totally blanked. I guess the natural response is to say that you can't really blame these people; after all, it's possible that Dan wanted to mug them or do something else horrible to them, and their best form of defence was to ignore him (a bit ironic when you think about it). Regardless, in Dan's eyes they were plain rude to him; they had shown him absolutely no respect regardless of the fact that he was polite and was only trying to help. The question on his mind is, therefore, why should he show respect to adults when they show no respect to him?

Dan's not the only one to find himself in this position. Jane likes hanging out at the city centre with her friends. She said she likes to go round the shops to see what's new and at times buy one or two things. They then like to go to one of the coffee bars for a drink and a sandwich or something else to eat. She cannot however comprehend why the shop assistants are so rude to them, continually hassling her and her friends to move on away from the shop. Why whenever they went for drinks they were told to leave almost before they'd even finished their drinks. Why people keep giving them funny looks when they hang about laughing and talking. Why people moved away from them as if they were diseased when there walked around from shop to shop. After all, they weren't doing anything wrong, just hanging out and having fun. So why, she wondered, were they being treated with such disdain?

I was specifically surprised about Jane's story and mentioned it to a couple of friends with teenage daughters, who both said their daughters had faced similar situations. These stories are far from uncommon in Milton Keynes and across the country today and the truth is that they are just the tip of the iceberg of the growing tendency that we have to treat young people with disrespect these days.

Possibly it's because we are scared of them and no longer know-how to engage with them. However, I believe we are sending them a very strange message and we are showing them a total lack of respect, treating them all as if they are guilty gangsters, but wondering why they show very little respect to us in return. Could it be that, just like most other people, they are simply responding to us?

The funny thing is that on the other extreme it is becoming the norm to show an extraordinary kind of respect to toddlers and young children. At times we seem to punctuate our every sentence, when talking to toddlers, with the word "please". It is not uncommon to hear a parent talking to a child that is being naught or perhaps about to run into the road, saying, "Johnny, please don't run into the road!" Wouldn't it be nice if we could show half this respect to our teenagers?

Moving from A to B: Redways

*Every day is a journey
And the journey itself is home.*
Matsuo Basho

I understand that there are places in Milton Keynes where there are people who never leave the estates they live on, or at least only do so on rare occasion and certainly never go into the city centre. It's quite difficult for me to fully comprehend this as, though I have a couple of friends on my estate who I drop by to visit from time to time, and stop for a quick chat with my neighbours when I see them; and although I spend a fair amount of time at home, unless I'm going for a walk around the woods, once I'm outdoors I tend to get in my car to drive to the local shops, to go to the city centre, the other side of Milton Keynes or indeed somewhere outside of Milton Keynes ranging from places such as Bedfordshire, to Cambridge to Northampton. (When going to London or Birmingham or places like that, I'm more inclined to park at the station and take a train.) A few times a year I also have the opportunity to get on a plane to go to Europe, the States or someone else. It's difficult for me to understand how people could live on an estate and hardly ever travel outside it.

One of the reasons, I understand, is that a number of people who fit this profile do not have cars. This may be because they don't want one or could possibly be a question of affordability. I can however say that, as previously highlighted, not having a car in Milton Keynes does very much limit mobility, specifically as our bus services are quite limited with buses on average passing a route every *half hour*.

A feature that we do have, that I very much appreciate and hope would make a marked difference, are the redway routes – a unique feature in Milton Keynes. The redway routes allow people to walk or cycle across most of Milton Keynes without going on the main roads. If you've ever been to London or Cambridge (which are major cycling cities) during the rush hours you will recognise how dangerous it can be for cyclists to cycle on the roads and how frustrating and annoying it can be for drivers to have cyclists in front of them when driving. A system that enables people to cycle on separate routes is awesome. I'm not, however, sure that the redways are being used as much as you would expect. Possibly because we are more inclined to use our cars than bikes, but more pertinently because there are questions about how safe the redways are. More significantly, if you are walking, with each grid square being approximately a kilometre apart, it is quite a distance walking from one estate to the next. Indeed, I used to go to a church not far from where I live. It would take me 3 minutes to get there by car, but 20 minutes to walk. On a nice day I did enjoy walking for the exercise, but it was nice to know that I had a choice and didn't have to walk in the rain.

I don't believe that anything can be done about the distances; however, I would like people to feel safer using the redways. Critically, the redways are sheltered by trees and the lighting is quite poor. I'm not aware of any incidents, but if there is a perception that they are not safe, then people are not inclined to use them. However, I believe if more people were to start to use them, people would grow to feel safer and more secure using them.

ASPIRATIONS

Going back to the fact that while most people in Milton Keynes are highly mobile, with a significant portion either living in Milton Keynes but working elsewhere or on the other end of the spectrum working in Milton Keynes, but living elsewhere. The fact that there are people who rarely travel outside of a small part of Milton Keynes does raise a number of questions.

Do they stay within the limited area because they do not have the economic means and transport to visit out of the area? Do they have any reason to want to travel outside of the area, are they actually aware of what actually exists outside of the area or are they in fact simply satisfied within the space they occupy? Do they have any awareness of what lies outside of the area they live in: the opportunities and challenges that the wider community presents and the best ways to access the opportunities and deal with challenges? If it is that they are actually happy within the area that they occupy and don't have any desire to travel outside of it, is this because they have everything they need within the area and don't have a need for anything outside of it? Are they satisfied and relatively fulfilled within that area? If so there is possibly a lot for us to learn from them! Regardless, as this is their environment and what their lives are centred around, what can be done to ensure that their aspirations are met and that they have fulfilled lives?

The fact I mention that these people live in a confined area, may lead people to believe that they don't have aspirations. I would, however, dispute this. Their more immediate aspirations may be quite different from those of the person whose aspiration is for their children to go to university, get a good job, buy a nice house and nice car, but again, looking at things from Maslow's perspective, I believe they definitely have aspirations.

I think the key things they want may translate differently, but are basically still the same. So they also want comfortable homes to live in with reasonably comfortable lives. The best for their children and the rest of their families. Usually nothing exorbitant. Unfortunately, though their wishes are usually far from exorbitant, sadly some of these aspirations will remain unfulfilled and out of reach unless they are supported in attaining them.

Pandora in a Complex World of Opportunities

And I know that it's a wonderful world
But I can't feel it right now,
I thought I was doing well but I just want to cry now,
James Morrison – Wonderful World, Album: Undiscovered

There is a growing perception that if you live in England the only thing to stop you from succeeding is yourself. I will add, especially if you live in an entrepreneur environment like Milton Keynes with growing employment opportunities.

Yes, as a young person you are told that you can be anything you want. I don't believe we are given clear maps to navigate the systems, and not everyone does.

The truth is that the world has become quite complex with all the choices now available to us. At the most basic level, even shopping is much more complex, with dozens of different teas or coffees to choose from. For a television do you go for plasma or LCD and, by the way, what screen size do you need? Is bigger better? Yet there are people trying to live a relatively simple life who are faced with all those complexities. Even then, if you know how to access and assess them, then all is well and good. There's at least one website that provides you with price comparisons across the main supermarkets of the main products through which you can shop online and get your groceries at the best price. Then there is the pricerunner website to help you determine what electronic goods best suit your needs and the best place to buy them. This is one of benefits of the internet if you have proper access to it and all the other tools that equip us for effective navigation.

There are also those who I believe just find something to hang on to and just hold on tight because it "works". Potentially wanting to move forward onto something better, but not knowing how to move forward, scared to let go of what they have got in order to try.

However, they are not realising that nothing in the world stands still – if you are not moving forward you will ultimately move backwards. While there are people who have made a conscious decision not to get caught up in the chase after financial riches and are content with a life that provides them with the bare necessities, I believe there is next to no one who wants to be poor and live off the system. As mentioned previously, while there may be (and are in fact) those who abuse the system, I have previously highlighted how difficult it is to live off the system. It is therefore a fallacy to assume that people make a conscious choice to do so.

Then you have the people who have fallen off i.e. the people who don't work because they can't work for health reasons. They are often people on incapacity benefits. Rightly or wrongly (dependent on the perspective from which you view things) there are single parents who do not believe it appropriate to leave small children to go out and work.

Possibly more pertinent is the case of people who are caught up and stuck. Stuck because they find the systems complex and do not know how to navigate and find their way through the maze to move upwards. Our system, even in the 21st century, is still quite complex and requires the knowledge of which form to fill for what, and the forms are quite complex such that one would often feel better off sticking with what one is used to.

But worse still is the situation of the person trying to navigate the world's complexities while facing his or her own internal complexities. I don't know about you, but I've found that the problem presented is often not the real problem and often there is a need to spend time unravelling things. For instance I saw a young man on telly a few weeks ago who was on drugs. He stole to feed his habit. In the interview he explained how he was sexually abused as a child. There was no one for him to talk to about the problem and he eventually used drugs to abate the pain. This grown man, who was in his late thirties, started to cry; telling the story brought the pain flooding back. He needed a fix to gain some relief from the pain. He felt that no one had ever been there to help him. He felt trapped.

Possibly more complex is the story of Sarah. Sarah was depressed. Her house was a mess - she was a mess. Because she was so depressed she didn't go out and talk to anyone. Because she spoke to no one she felt isolated and alone sitting in her mess and she became more of a mess. She thought that would solve her problems, but the problem was more complex - she was in a cycle that needed to be broken.

How she got there I do not know. Who is to blame is totally irrelevant. The important thing is she needed a way out before it got too late. Possibly someone to talk to who could guide her, step-by-step, through things would make a world of difference to her. The only thing is if you or I saw her with her child in a buggy looking a bit untidy and distracted as he cries, we would most likely just wonder why she was such a bad mother.

WELFARE SYSTEM

The best way to put more money in people's wallets
is to leave it there in the first place
EDWIN FEULNER

The British welfare system dates back to the 1940s and the number of people who have benefited from it over time is immeasurable. Unfortunately, the welfare system now presents major challenges that the government needs to tackle at some point in time, hopefully sooner rather than later. At its foundation, I believe the welfare system remains positive and well-intentioned.

I can hardly begin to imagine the number of people who have been saved from destitution by the welfare system. Who have been helped during difficult periods by having the welfare system to fall back on for a short period while they get themselves together after falling into difficult times. I would therefore never advocate for the removal of the welfare system.

I do, however, believe that there are serious problems with the welfare system in its current form. To my thinking it doesn't seem right that a person on income support can be better off than someone out working, but indeed it does happen.

People are often faced with a moral dilemma as to whether they should pick themselves up and take a job that would pay them less than what they obtain while on benefits, or continue to live on benefits until such a time as they can find work which will pay them better (if that will ever occur). In discussions with people when I mention this, the view often expressed is that a sense of self-esteem or moral obligation should drive people to work regardless of the potential loss of income. However, as already mentioned, if an individual's lower-level needs are yet to be met, then these are less pertinent.

So in my mind, for as long as you can be better off on income-related benefits than when you are out working, the welfare system provides a crutch and serves as a challenge to the very people that it is aimed at supporting.

Support – Rights and Responsibilities

Give a man a fish and you feed him for a day.
Teach a man to fish and you feed him for a lifetime.
Chinese Proverb

In society these days, we tend to focus a lot on rights. I believe that everyone does have certain rights. Specifically the rights to decent standards of living and housing – most especially if we live in the "developed" world. At the same time we are first and foremost responsible for our own individual lives.

When it comes to community change, people within a local area will, however, need support to turn things around in order to take responsibility to make things happen. I believe that more often than not, they are ready to do something to achieve the things they want. Sometimes they do need to be reminded of their responsibilities in making the changes.

I believe the real problem is when we assume that we know what they want and need and come along and impose things on people in a way that does not really work. At work we talk about hearts and minds. I believe the same should apply when we go into communities to help them effect changes. In fact more often than not, with a little support and guidance the people who actually know themselves and the other people within their neighbourhoods are best able to effect the changes required themselves.

Just as they have responsibilities for themselves, we have responsibilities towards them, as our lives and destinies are all intertwined. When I lived on the outskirts of London and received the news that my journey into work was going to be disrupted because someone had jumped on the track, my initial thoughts were of annoyance – wondering why they could not have found a different way of committing suicide. But as I stood on the train platform or found alternative ways into central London by bus or some other means, I would begin to calculate the costs to business and the economy as a whole caused by the disruption. I would then go on to think of what could have been said to the person in question to prevent them from taking such a drastic action.

That person will always have been somebody else's next door neighbour. And maybe someone could have done or said that special thing to prevent that person from tripping over the edge. But maybe the person seemed all right and without any need of support. But a smile or a quick hello has never hurt anyone.

Over time, there have been occasions when I have had neighbours who have appeared not to be very friendly, but I've found that when I've constantly smiled at them and mumbled hello, they've responded eventually.

Communication and Joint Working to Succeed:
(Support- Right Type, Effect of Support)

"Communication is the key to education,
understanding and peace."
James Bryce

Everyone is in a hurry these days. I believe where we see problems we tend to look for the quickest way of solving them so that we can move on to the next thing or simply just continue with our busy lives. So I'm not saying for one minute that we ignore the things that are wrong. A key problem, however, is that we don't seem to take the time to understand the root cause of the problem, so we deal with symptoms and not solutions for the real issue.

We come up with formulas based on what our intellect tells us will work or what has worked elsewhere without getting to the root of the unique set of circumstances in a specified situation. The simplest way of doing this would be to engage with the people with the problem in order to attain an understanding of what they think is wrong and what they actually want. Unfortunately, however, we tend to believe that we know what is best for other people, work out our formulas to put these things in place and end up getting frustrated when they do not have the desired effect or are unappreciated.

Take for instance the childcare training that was provided for some of the residents of Netherfield. I believe this was a very positive initiative. While parents have a natural capability to look after their children, such a course added to those natural skills. The expectation was that the mothers would complete the course, become certified child carers, and then start working on that basis. They did complete the course, but they did not go on to be certified, perhaps because this has wider implications that link into the issues of the welfare system. It would be easy to question the decisions of the mothers not to become certified, however, if someone had spoken to them before the course had started the problem may have come to light and a different approach may have been taken which would have avoided the disappoint of not having the statistics at the end or, alternatively, the course could have been run as it was, but with a different end objective of simply ensuring that the parents had the adequate skills to properly look after their children.

So let's have formulas, but let's use them as frameworks which we adapt to meet needs based on communications that provide an understanding of actual needs within an area. Otherwise we will be like doctors who conclude that every patient that walks through the door has the flu, simply because they sneeze!

As it stands there are around 50 agencies that work in Nether-field, 60 that work in Beanhill. I commend all their hard work and efforts – I really do. I guess no one is more frustrated than they are by the limits to what they have achieved to date – or maybe I'm just impatient, but I really wish that they had been able to achieve more over the time they have been working within the areas.

I was pleased to hear that a Place Check programme took place at the Lakes Estate whereby the local people and visitors to the estate were asked some basic questions about what they liked/wanted and disliked about the area. I'm aware that consultation is very time-consuming, but it does increase the probability of gaining the buy-in of local people, involvement and actually meeting their needs. I hope and believe that similar exercises will take place in the other parts of Milton Keynes targeted for regeneration.

This is important because if agencies have a clear understanding from the people of what it is that they really want and need, maybe this will better enable them to work together to meet these focused needs – by allocating responsibilities for specific objectives and ensuring that their services do not unnecessarily overlap and that, at the same time, there are no gaps.

I believe that we in Milton Keynes are fortunate to have so many agencies working here, however agencies are often over-burdened by targets from their funders, which limits their effectiveness. Sadly, the focus on target often makes it seem as if they are undergoing tick-box exercises which are not really people-focused.

It's nice to know that there are inter-agency organisations working in Milton Keynes. However, I'm not sure that anyone has overall responsibility for issues. I also suspect that there is a lot of duplication because everyone does what they do and no one actually gives way when they find that someone else is already doing what they are doing. After all, this is what they are targeted to do.

It would be ideal if, on identifying the real needs with an area, that overall responsibility for issues could be allocated to specific agencies who could work alongside other agencies to fulfil them, and ultimately, avoiding unnecessary duplication and ensuring accountability. This would go a long way towards achieving the necessary results within the areas.

So Who Comes Next?

The Shortest Distance between New Friends
Is a Smile
Anon

Milton Keynes' population has grown in diversity over time and as it continues to grow so will its diversity. I believe it will continue to attract people from other major cities across the country.

I'm conscious that, through Invest MK, there seems to be an objective of attracting larger businesses into Milton Keynes. As they do, will the employees of these organisations come with them or choose to stay where they currently are? Even if they do bring a large proportion of their employees with them, the presence of these organisations should still lead to new jobs and business opportunities for local people.

Five years ago when I moved to Milton Keynes from London a major pull factor was the cheaper cost of housing and room space in Milton Keynes. Due to both its success and the general rise in housing costs across the south east, Milton Keynes is no longer as cheap as it used to be, but I still believe that it's an attractive place to live in.

All in all, I'm not really sure who will come next. I do, however, hope that whoever comes will be willing to make an effort to integrate with us and that the local authorities will have made adequate plans for their arrival into our community.

MIDDLE CHILD SYNDROME

I'm a typical middle child. I'm the mediator.
The one that makes everything OK,
puts their own needs aside to make sure everybody's happy.
It's hard to change your nature,
even with years and years of therapy.
JENNIFER JASON LEIGH

In Milton Keynes we have the areas earmarked for regeneration, the relatively new areas, and the rest, built in the periods in between. Here, as in most places, we have the people who are really struggling; those who are doing okay, and those who are just getting by. Those living in the areas built in between and those who just get by are just like middle children.

There has been a fair amount of study around the personality traits that we develop on the basis of our birth order. There are numerous traits that can be mentioned when you look at it from the psychological perspective, such as the fact that firstborns are typically highly structured; middle children are not good at making commitments, while lastborns like to be the centre of attention.

I'm not going to go into the psychology, I'm going to talk about a few basic observations I've made with my family and those of friends. When my sisters, friends and most of the people I know have been pregnant with their first child, they have got very excited. They've read every book and magazine possible and followed the instructions through to the T. They've followed this through when they've actually had the baby. They've breastfed. They've been into Mothercare, Mamas & Papas or wherever and bought all those little things that have very little real value. If baby sneezed they ran to the doctor's and demanded something be done. Come child number two, yes there is excitement and joy, but since it's been done before, people aren't so reliant on the books. We've worked things out. We recognise that at times babies sneeze, cough and get sick, but it's not all life-threatening. We've come to recognise that we don't always have to buy the most expensive clothes for babies as they soon grow out of them. Besides, they can use some of the clothes of the firstborn that are still in very good condition. Then we get to our last child: this is our last chance. We're not going to have another one, so we might as well get everything new. This child will always be the baby to be spoilt by all.

The second child or any other child born in between the first and the last child are "victims" of what I refer to as "middle children syndrome". Please don't get the wrong impression, I'm not saying that they are unimportant to their parents, but in comparative terms middle children get far less attention. Significantly, the middle child syndrome affects all aspects of society.

Take the school system in its more traditional format. For example, typically children who struggle within the system are classified as children with special needs and schools tend to pay a lot of attention to their needs in order to help them to keep up. In more recent years we have come to recognise children that we classify as gifted, because they are academically clever. We therefore pay extra attention to them and put special activities in place to help ensure that they are stimulated and reach their full potential. On the other hand you have the children who are academically average. Often they may feel like they are victims of the middle child syndrome as they are just left to get on with things. Sometimes they feel that they don't get much help, even when they ask for it. This is evident from a young man who told me that he didn't enjoy school because the teachers only paid attention to the clever ones.

The middle child syndrome doesn't stop here. I believe it extends its tentacles into all levels of society – and I'm just as guilty as the next person. These figures are not scientific, but it could be said that in society, 25% of people are faced with real serious issues, 25% are doing all right, but the remaining 50% sit in the middle group and are struggling to keep their heads above water and cope. Like typical middle children, we pay little attention to them, unless they fall. There is a possibility that they may end up feeling frustrated and resentful, because their needs are seen as secondary.

Just as while those struggling may need special attention, those doing okay are not to be neglected until they end up struggling. I sincerely believe that poverty in parts of Africa and Asia is a serious problem that we cannot ignore. At the same time, I don't believe that we can afford to ignore the economic and social poverty in our own backyard.

I've heard debates about whether we really have poverty in the UK, when compared to certain parts of Africa. The real challenge is to raise the standards across the board – for those struggling and those getting by, to the levels of those doing well, while recognising that they will not stand still but continue to move forwards. Simultaneously we should continue supporting those in poorer areas of Asian and Africa. We can't really afford to do one without the other.

PERCEPTION

What you see and hear
depends a good deal on where you are standing;
it also depends on what sort of person you are.
C. S. LEWIS

For all the people highlighted, I believe the biggest challenge that they face relates to perception. For the original inhabitants, there is the perception that they did not exist pre-1967 and that, possibly, they do not have their own unique needs and identity. That people do not recognise that they feel marginalised due to the development of the new areas with little focus on their own needs, especially as key facilities were refocused from their areas such as the station and Bletchley and the shopping centre and the impact of the close of the Mill on the Wolverton economy.

For the people in the less economically prosperous areas there must be a lot of frustration that the only times people tend to remember them is when something negative happens. Attitudes and perceptions that could easily make people give up and take a "Que Sera, Sera" attitude (whatever may be will be). It is possible that crime is higher in these areas, but are the people who live within each of the communities the ones actually committing the crimes or is it possible that other people come into the areas to commit crimes? That people from outside notice the economic deprivation in the areas with drugs and other things that give the areas a negative reputation?

I believe that, sadly, economic deprivation attracts crime as people tend to prey on the "weak". Even if it is people within the area who cause the problems, what percentage of the local population do they represent? For instance, I understand that there are up to 1,000 young people on the Lakes Estate. Around 40 of these young people spend a lot of time in the square generally making noise and making people feel uncomfortable, but, most importantly giving young people as a whole within the area a bad name.

If as I believe, most of the people living in these places want a safe, secure environment for themselves and their families, it is not logical in my mind that they are any happier with rubbish being dumped in the areas than anyone else would be.

It's unfortunate to say, but once in a while when a neighbour or two leaves rubbish outside for collection, someone else's cat or dog smells something interesting and makes a hole in the bag in order to investigate. On a windy day this leads to rubbish being blown all over the place – inclusive of the front of my previously neat and clean house. I find this annoying. The situation is even worse when people leave their rubbish out a few days early – possibly because they are not going to be around on collection day or perhaps for some other reason. The fortunate thing is that this does not happen very often where I live and only one or two people do it.

For young people it must be difficult when people are always putting you down, complaining about the way you dress, the fact that you spend times hanging out in groups with your friends, the quality of education that you are provided with and yet never take the time to stop and talk to you to gain an understanding of how you think and feel.

All in all, I believe that there is good and bad in everyone, but it is what we nurture that ultimately determines what they become or possibly what it is that we actually see. The next questions are therefore: Who is responsible for nurturing and bringing out the good, and what can we as individuals do to help?

So How Successful are We?

"As long as there is poverty in the world I can never be rich,
even if I have a billion dollars.
As long as diseases are rampant and millions of people in this world
cannot expect to live more than twenty-eight or thirty years,
I can never be totally healthy,
even if I just got a good checkup at the Mayo Clinic.
I can never be what I ought to be until you are what you ought to be.
This is the way our world is made.
No individual or nation can stand out boasting of being independent.
We are all interdependent."
DR. MARTIN LUTHER KING, JR.

Within the context of their ways of life and aspirations, I believe these people all want the best for the family – starting with food, shelter, and a loving, secure environment. Their requirements may not extend to the bigger things like travelling the world, owning a big house or being the managing director of a company, but who is to say that these are the things that really amount to success?

Research actually shows that *things* do not ultimately make us happy. Research shows that many a time they actually make us unhappy. Though I guess what we see in the media is often skewed, if the reports on celebrities, who materially are the most successful people on earth, are accurate, they are actually a desperate miserable bunch of people who are totally unfulfilled.

So if we have all the material things in the world that we could possibly want - good jobs, successful businesses – does this make us happy? If it does that is fantastic, but how about the people who surround us? If they are in deep need, how successful are we?

So there is a question left on my mind as to how we help these people to attain the things they really want and need. We cannot afford to leave them behind – it is not an option.

Until their basic aspirations are met, it will be quite difficult for people to start thinking about travelling the world (or even the country) or Milton Keynes as a whole. It will be difficult for them to raise their aspirations to think about work that is enjoyable and possibly more fulfilling, and the fact that it is more important to go out and work even if they would be worse off financially if they worked than they are by sitting at home on benefits. Most especially if there is a relatively high proportion of people in their environment who are not out working in jobs that they find fulfilling.

If we take the time to help and support those around us, we may learn a lot in return and become much more fulfilled in our own right. Only then do I believe that we will be truly successful.

WHO HAS RESPONSIBILITY?

THE POLITICAL SYSTEM

"The true leader serves. Serves people. Serves their best interests, and in doing so will not always be popular, may not always impress. But because true leaders are motivated more by loving concern than a desire for personal glory, they are willing to pay the price."
EUGENE B. HABECKER

Beyond the natural abilities that we as individuals have, we can also control and shape our own destinations. The biggest, all-encompassing human influences on the way we live are all the different politicians who make up the political systems that invariably determine or influence all the other systems within which we live.

Milton Keynes comes under the unitary authority of Milton Keynes Council. This in effect means that it is a single-tier local government, as opposed to the more traditional two-tier local government structure of England, and as such has responsibility for almost all local government functions within their area.

Since the 2005 local elections, when the Liberal Democrats lost a number of seats, Milton Keynes Council has ceased to have a party with a ruling majority. Following the May 3, 2007 elections the council's 51 seats have been divided between the Liberal Democrats, Conservatives, Labour and an Independent in the ratio of 45%, 29.55, 25.5% and 2%. respectively i.e. Lib Dem 22, Conservative 15, Labour 13, Independent 1. As there are a number of seats up for re-election this year, the ratios may change. To be honest it's hard to keep up as there seem to be elections for council seats almost every year. I believe this limits the stability of the Council and its ability to make long-term effective planning.

Whether or not it is a good thing that we don't currently have a party with a ruling majority may depend on who you talk to and the topic of the day. From a liberal democratic perspective I guess it could be said that they can't just get on and do what they need to do to run the town without rallying for support from at least one of the other parties, who could possibly over-politicise things and become difficult. (Decisions voted on require at least 50% of the votes in order to be accepted.) The other parties may, however, view things differently e.g. from the perspective that they are currently in the position to prevent the Liberal Democrats from (in their view) doing things that are not to the advantage of the people.

When I first moved to Milton Keynes, I didn't really give much thought to the political system. I was not politically unaware; I've always been fully aware of what goes on at a national level politically and my Thursday evening television viewing regularly follows a pattern of watching the news, followed by *Question Time*, concluding with *This Week*. But as far as Milton Keynes is concerned, I was aware that the strategic management of the Council was in the hands of a Liberal Democrat-led majority council. I knew that we were represented in Parliament by two Labour councillors (changing in 2006 to one Labour and one Conservative). I also did my bit by voting in all the elections – local and general.

I was also unaware of the fact that we have Parish Councils with responsibilities for some local decisions, until I had a good look at the breakdown of my Council Tax bill and noticed that there was an amount which goes towards the running of the Parish Council.

THE POLITICIANS – I THINK THEY ARE ACTUALLY HUMAN

"Almost all our faults are more pardonable than the methods we employ to hide them."
FRANCOIS DE LA ROCHEFOUCAULD

Last year I was invited to observe the running of a local council meeting. It's quite sad to say that it did not paint a very positive impression in my mind, as an unreasonable amount of time seemed to be spent bickering, in spite of the fact that there were a number of guests who had come along because of their concerns over some possible changes to a few of the local schools. On reflection, it would be fair to say that only a few of the councillors behaved in a manner that I found distasteful, but sadly it is their behaviour that stood out in my mind and made me wonder why they were actually doing the job.

In many ways the job of a politician (at whatever level) is quite thankless and I wonder what motivates them to go for the job. At the same time I wonder what the real qualifications are for becoming a politician or, possibly more pertinently, what qualifies a politician to represent the people as I believe that is the most critical role of a politician. I know that if you look at any local authority website you find information listed which will include things like not having a criminal record, living in the area for a certain number of years etc. However, there does not seem to be anything about motivation – is it just assumed that anyone applying to take up a political office naturally cares about the people? I personally believe that this is crucial – after all that's largely what it is about isn't it? And this is what I think would motivate a politician to press on if and when they are insulted or abused for not doing a good enough job or doing it in a way that is not to the liking of the vocal majority. On the other hand, there is nothing written to say that their motivation should not be greed, selfish ambitions or to be known and be popular. I guess there is a question as to how these criteria would be accessed and continually tested to see if it was actually being met, even if it did exist.

It can't be the money – they are not paid a salary for what they do. They only receive an allowance, which can only be stretched so far. If they become Councillors for the prestige, I think they would soon become disillusioned and quiet. We don't give our politicians that much respect. Very rarely do we stop to thank them for the things they do and get right, but we have no hesitation in condemning them for the slightest mistake they make. I recognise that I'm not entirely innocent myself. It was a visit to MK theatre for the MK Gala 40th Birthday celebration that brought this home to me.

After the main event, there were two ladies who sang in the foyer. They sang a lot of music from the '70s and '80s, which drew quite a crowd of people who came to sing along, dance, or just listen. Within the crowd I saw one of the local councillors, quietly standing alone, listening. I've noticed this person regularly attending social events in Milton Keynes, but this day s/he was standing alone, taking in the atmosphere – not talking to anyone, and no one talking to her. Now I'm not saying that there is anything wrong with people standing alone; a number of people feel comfortable this way and even prefer it, but this is someone who, regardless of whatever the odds may be, has helped to make Milton Keynes what it is. Someone who most people in Milton Keynes would recognise. But throughout the evening, I saw only one person venture over to this person to say thank you, hello, hi or even give a little smile. So if the motivation for this person was ever prestige, it doesn't seem to me that we are providing this and with the fighting amongst colleagues, it doesn't seem that it is being obtained at that level either. So there must be some other motivation.

I concluded that this person, like all her colleagues, genuinely cares. I doubt if any of them really understands all the issues. I guarantee that they will make mistakes from time to time. They will never please everyone – it's not humanly possible. But I am convinced that most, if not all of them, passionately care. Otherwise it would be insane for them to go through what they go through for the return they get, because I believe the only real return they get is the knowledge that they make a difference in some small way for a few people from time to time and that can only mean something if you care, because of those few people only fewer still will come back with a thank you or a smile as opposed to further complaints about what is not as opposed to what is.

I find the often childish behaviour of politicians tiresome, especially when they attend public meetings and heckle speakers – I'm not sure how they believe this effectively represents the people. However, I must say I can only think of one politician in Milton Keynes whose attitudes and behaviours indicate a total lack of care and concern for the people represented. Most of the time, regardless of what happens in Council meetings, local councillors seem to work tirelessly within the local areas to meet the needs of the local people

As they care for the same thing – the people of Milton Keynes – I genuinely don't understand why they spend so much time bickering and trying to pull each other down instead of jointly focusing their energy on the common goals.

A Qangoland

*"It's not hard to make decisions
when you know what your values are."*
Roy Disney

Although Milton Keynes has a clear political structure with an elected local council and parish councils, people still continually ask who actually runs Milton Keynes. This is because there are a number of Qangos in Milton Keynes that have responsibility for a number of key areas. Just in case you don't know what a Qango is, it is an acronym for a Quasi Autonomous Non Government Organisation, now more commonly referred to as Non-Departmental Public Bodies (NDPB). Definitions aside, the important thing is how they come about and what they do.

I'm not going to go into details about all the Quangos in Milton Keynes, more than anything because in truth it is actually quite difficult to identify them. The most important ones to be aware of however are: English Partnership/Milton Keynes Partnership; Milton Keynes Economic and Learning and Parks Trust

Milton Keynes Partnership was set up by English Partnership to bring together representatives from the health, community and business sectors along with independent representatives to capitalise and strengthen existing working relationships across the city and use their powers to drive forward and deliver new development. I believe it is therefore fair to say that Milton Keynes Partnership is responsible for the implementation of the Central Government growth agenda within Milton Keynes.

Milton Keynes Economic & Learning Partnership is aimed at ensuring that "In 2034 Milton Keynes will be a major free-standing City, with a diverse, high-value business base offering well-paid employment opportunities to all those living within the City".[12] It aims to achieve this by developing a diverse and broadly based economy, a strong representation of knowledge-based workers, and a thriving centre for knowledge-based industries.

The Parks Trust was set up as a registered charity by Milton Keynes Development Corporation to manage and protect the parks and other green spaces.

Although there is a lot of controversy over Quangos due to their non-elected nature, I believe the biggest frustration about them within Milton Keynes is the lack of clarity over who has responsibility for what. To try and be fair on this, the committees that run the Qangos each generally include 3 elected members. Sadly, I believe I am unfortunately unable to add much more clarity on this as it is really difficult to get clear information on this area.

AGENCIES

For every action
There is an equal and opposite government program
BOB WELLS

There are a large number of agencies working to support, develop and improve upon Milton Keynes. By agency, I refer to the many different organisations – voluntary, council or private – that work directly in different areas of the community ranging from education, skills and training, investment, financial services, housing, social and so on – in order to support the communities.

It is difficult to give a precise number, but it is fair to say that there are quite a large number of agencies operating within Milton Keynes. I have been made to understand that in Netherfield there are up to 50 different agencies, while Beanhill has up to 60. Unfortunately, I don't have a breakdown to understand precisely who they are and what they do: it's too daunting a task for me to undertake at this point in time. I do, however, believe that they are all well-intentioned organisations.

A number of the agencies that work within the community are in fact part of the council, such as Extended Schools and Surestart, together with other public-sector bodies such as the Fire Service and the Police. I would estimate that at least 10% of the agencies are actually public sector bodies.

The vast majority of agencies are, however, voluntary organisations. There are currently around 1400 voluntary/charitable organisations operating in or around Milton Keynes. The services that they cover include advice and information, advocacy, economic development, emotional support, housing and hostels, heritage, international development, faith groups and places of worship, community development and planning and sports and recreation, to mention a few.

The agencies aim to support all members of the community, with some specialising on specific areas such as black and ethnic minorities, senior citizens, the homeless, young people, people of particular religions, faiths and cultures, children, and the environment.

All in all it is safe to say that the different agencies aim to represent all areas of the community.

MEDIA

"The man who does not read good books
has no advantage over the man who cannot read them."
MARK TWAIN

While the Government at different levels has the responsibility for creating and implementing policies which have a marked impact on our way of life, it is the media that highlights to us areas of policy and its implications that they believe are important for us to be made aware of. The media often takes on the role of ensuring that the Government is accountable to us, by reporting on its activities – both on a professional and personal level. They also keep us informed of what is going on within the wider society from a business, social, economic and cultural perspective.

For a place of its size, I believe Milton Keynes has rather extensive media coverage.

Before I moved to Milton Keynes, I used to get a friend to send the then main newspaper, *The Citizen*, to me. This was mainly so that I could review the property section, but also so that I could maintain an understanding of what was going on within the town. There is a now a second newspaper, *MK News*, which provides *The Citizen* with some healthy competition.

We also have a few good business magazines such as *Inside News*, *Business MK*, the Chamber's magazine, *Vision*, together with a glossy lifestyle magazine called *Inside Living Milton Keynes*.

In addition to coverage by BBC Three Counties Radio we also have our own exclusive local radio station, Horizon Radio, which provides both local and national news and entertainment.

We have at least three major news and general information websites: the official website, MKWeb, MiltonKeynes.com, and *The Citizen's* website, MiltonKeynes.co.uk. Something that is possibly quite unique is the fact that we also have an award-winning online television station, Ask MK TV, which is focused on TV Style video advertising and local news coverage.

What if God was one of Us?

For I was hungry and you gave me something to eat,
I was thirsty and you gave me something to drink,
I was a stranger and you invited me in,
I needed clothes and you clothed me,
I was sick and you looked after me,
I was in prison and you came to visit me.'
Matthew 25:35-36 from The Holy Bible: New International Version

The Church used to be one of the first places that people would go to for help. From this perspective, it's great that there are a significant number of churches in Milton Keynes, at least 3 mosques, and a Sikh temple, amongst other religious organisations. It's also good to know that a number of the churches and other bodies meet together as Interfaith MK.

The sad thing, however, is that what is publicised about the Church and religion in general these days is often negative. There is a focus on what the Church disagrees with within society and what they stand against as opposed to the core of what Christianity and, I believe, most religions, stand for.

Speaking from a Christian perspective, I can say without hesitation that the primary message of the Bible is love, and although there are times when we get caught up in debates about the rights and wrongs in society, the message still remains love. I hope that like me, when people hear of these groups they think of them as places of love and support – ideally as a first port of call and, if not, at least as a last resort. I also hope that we as members of these bodies always remember to show the face of love to the people of Milton Keynes and beyond and continually stop to think about our actions – what would Jesus have done? Would He be proud of the way in which I have responded to people today?

As a Christian, I believe that Christians and the Church as well as other religious groups in Milton Keynes have major roles to play in society. I don't believe that I would feel any different if I was not a Christian if I felt that the Church was playing an effective role. The truth is that I believe that while we try, being like most other people in society who are caught up with their day-to-day life – at times we miss the mark. Having said this, I believe that there are a high number of Christians who work for voluntary organisations that support community needs or that volunteer. However as a body, I believe that what we as the Church do is much more limited than before – possibly due to the separation between the State and Church.

The Church is no longer as directly linked to the State as it used to be but I still believe it has some influence on Government, which should be focused more on how to meet community needs than the other issues we often get caught up in.

I don't want to go into Church history, but historically the Church was directly linked to the State and most belonged or had an affiliation to the Church which gave it direct access to the people in order to help meet their needs. Indeed, prior to the introduction of welfare system the church played a large role in meeting the needs of the community.

There are religious groups that are involved in meeting community needs, but it seems that their focus is more often than not on those people that share their religious beliefs. It is not my intention to undermine this. I believe that everything that is done makes some difference. .

There are a lot of Churches that have set up international projects to help people in developing countries. I believe Christians have always had an involvement in this area, but I believe it has increased. This could be because of the media focus on the problems of the developing world because of our social responsibility.

This is good, important and relevant, as the fundamental message of the Bible is love - that we should love our neighbours ourselves. I don't have much knowledge about other religions; I believe their messages are not dissimilar. I therefore believe it is fundamental that people from different religious groups be involved in international projects, but as we do so I hope that it is not at the expense of our neighbours that live next door to us!

EDUCATION

"The function of education is to teach one to think intensively and to think critically ...
Intelligence plus character - that is the true goal education."
MARTIN LUTHER KING JR

In Milton Keynes there are a number of parent and toddler groups, 89 primary schools and 11 secondary schools (inclusive of five special schools)[13] with the overall numbers constantly growing as Milton Keynes expands. There's also a college, creatively called Milton Keynes College, and it is also home to the Open University. Cranfield University and the University of Buckinghamshire are in neighbouring towns.

Like most places, the work of educational institutions is an integral and increasingly integrated part of Milton Keynes' makeup –especially with the work of organisations such as Connexions and Countec which, amongst other things, link schools with the business community. Indeed, schools have always been an integral part of the community; it is inevitable. The role that they play has, however, evolved over time.

When I started school, both pupils and teachers tended to live in the vicinity. Teachers were known within the community and did not have to wait until a parent visited the school to have a discussion about problems. Parents largely tended to respect and back teachers when teachers presented problems with a pupil, and teachers had the authority to discipline pupils as they saw fit. By the time I left school things had markedly changed, and they changed even further in the following years. The population became more mobile, meaning that teachers no longer live in the local community as a rule of thumb. Where they do live in the local community, for data protection, health and safety, and other legislative reasons, they may be much more reluctant to openly express their concerns to the parents outside of school. It is no longer guaranteed that a parent will back a teacher when an issue arises with a pupil and teachers' ability to discipline pupils has been very much eroded, while, at the same time, pupils are very much more aware of their rights.

This has not, however, stopped teachers from caring, and doing their best to support pupils – even if perhaps (if they are anything like me), they may often feel unsupported, frustrated and concerned by the legislation and approach of both central government and local authorities. (The parents who appreciate what the schools do are less likely to provide the school with feedback than those who are either justly or unjustly dissatisfied). Regardless, over time, teachers have developed numerous initiatives to support pupils both within school hours and outside of them, such as breakfast clubs and after-school clubs.

It is somewhat annoying when the Government turns around and legislates that all schools should have responsibility for providing extended school facilities that cover after-school activities; access to specialist services; parenting and family support; and community access to school facilities. This puts formal responsibility on schools for the whole of the community without even taking cognisance of what is already being done. I, for one, am grateful for the work of teachers and the education system, even though I believe that regardless of their intentions, schools efforts and work are often thwarted by government legislation.

I doff my hat to the teachers who run the education system, as the education that we get goes a very long way to determine who we become. The teacher who believes in us can very easily compensate for the parent that doesn't – simply because they don't or perhaps because they don't understand or know any better.

One of the more inspiring films that I have watched as of late is a film called The Freedom Writers. It is based on a true-life situation in America, where a newly qualified teacher went to work for a school, teaching English to a class of pupils from diverse, enemy social backgrounds. A number of the pupils were members of not rival, but enemy, gangs. Against the odds, with a lack of support from her head of Department and limited support from the local authority (in the early days), she brought them to a place whereby they learnt that they were actually more alike than different. More significantly, she taught them the importance of who they were as individuals. Regardless of the odds of the outside world they were able to stand together more or less as a family. Today those pupils are all successful in their chosen careers.

I tell this story not to highlight the struggles of people from poorer social backgrounds, but to show, how the education system can positively impact pupils. Without her the pupils in question would have been left to simply drift through the system. It would have been nice if she, together with all other teachers, did not have to fight the odds to achieve results.

So on this note, I once more doff my hat to all the teachers who positively impact on young people. I've always believed that without them there would be no doctors, engineers, lawyers, accounts etc – can you see what I mean?

They would be more effective if we spent more time asking them what they need to be more effective, rather than simply spending time telling them what to do. Specifically those things that they are already doing.

WHAT ELSE CAN BE DONE?

The Heart of Milton Keynes

The Greatest treasures are those invisible to the eye
But found by the heart
Anon

People often say that Milton Keynes lacks heart. I'm not sure I fully understand why, but I suspect it's because we don't have a central landmark in the City Centre such as a cathedral or some other grand building.

Though this may be true, we do have a number of interesting landmarks. We also have a lot of beautiful artwork in the centre and across the city as a whole, especially within the older parts of the new town. The heartbeat of Milton Keynes is not always reflected in buildings and landmarks. The beat is actually strongest in the community activities and support shown by the people.

Because of the setup of Milton Keynes with the spread across a significant area, I don't believe a singular heart or heart beat is sufficient for us. After all, what would be the purpose of a singular city heartbeat, when there is a limit to the number of people who live in the Centre? To be effective it is important that there is a heartbeat in every area of the city.

Milton Keynes already has a number of little heartbeats, reflected in the lives and actions of the people. They are not always the healthiest heartbeats and even, when they are healthy, they still need to be nurtured and need to be developed in areas where heart is lacking.

The key question is how we bring the heartbeat to full life – to beat in harmony across the whole of the City.

Soul Town – A Call to Social Consciousness

You say Soul town,
Is the way it's all meant to be
And someday we'll build it all again.
When we've had enough of this emptiness
Far too much of this loneliness
We'll start afresh, raise is up, and grow.
From the song Soul Town by Ola Onabule (2004)

Let me tell you a little story. From time to time, I go to The Stables for a concert, but one that stands out in my mind was an Ola Onabule concert that I attended in 2006. His name caught my attention on the Stables event list and though I hadn't heard of him before the ticket prices were very reasonable, so I thought, why not? I asked a friend if he would like to come along and excitedly he said yes. He did know Onabule and was of the opinion that he was very good.

He was right! I was definitely not disappointed and I had a great time. I recommend him to anyone who really loves the soul music of the '80s and '90s. He was great when he sang an interactive soul train medley that took us on a walk through the soul era. However, the song that stands out most in my mind and really made me think was a song entitled Soul Town.

Soul Town, unsurprisingly, had a great soul beat that helped take you back in time as Ola sang about the soul era. It sounded quite nostalgic as he sang about how things were back in those days. Specifically, I remember the line: "What happened to all those dreams of peace, and understanding and harmony and brotherhood and love. Being together forever and ever." The only thing is as he sang this, he also kept singing, "This is not a love song, this is not nostalgia". This left me somewhat confused as I originally thought he was just reminiscing over the music. Subsequently, after the concert as he autographed my CD, I asked him, "If it's not nostalgia – what is it?" His simple response was "It's a call to social consciousness".

To make sure he meant what I thought he meant I thought I'd double-check the meaning. I'm going to dare to quote the definition that I found on Wikipedia which is "Social consciousness is consciousness shared within a society. It can also be defined as social awareness; to be aware of the problems that different societies and communities face on a day-to-day basis; to be conscious of the difficulties and hardships of society." In case you hadn't realised it, this is my call to social consciousness and this leads to the first point.

In earlier sections, I have attempted to start the process of creating an awareness of what is going on around us within our community. Have I succeeded? If you doubt the validity of what I say there are substantial statistics on Milton Keynes Social Atlas[14] which substantiate what I have said.

My focus has been Milton Keynes, but to some extent it could be anywhere and the principles could be applied anywhere as, although Milton Keynes has its own unique issues and circumstances, there are things that are common to any community if you look closely enough. I have presented issues from my perspective, but there is a reality that there is financial disparity, social issues and misunderstanding of young people everywhere. We may never be able to totally eliminate the social issues and problems of the world, but I believe we can at least try to minimise them – and I believe this starts with social consciousness.

Decoding the Media

"Most writers regard truth as their most valuable possession,
and therefore are most economical in its use."
Mark Twain

I don't for one minute believe that people have really stopped caring. I do, however, believe that we have become very busy; often too busy to see beyond what we are told – predominantly by the media. The fact that we still care is evident by our response to the Asian tsunami when people went out of their way to give money in support of the people affected by the disaster and the number of people on holiday in the area who used the rest of their holidays to help with the cleanup. By the number of people who have since gone back on holiday for the primary purpose of helping the area to recover. The fact that we still care is also evident by the response to the Make Poverty History campaign. By the response to poverty in Africa, with numerous people supporting projects, sponsoring children, or going to work on projects. These are a few of the indications that we definitely still care – very much indeed.

My concern is that we are less aware of the circumstances of the people in our immediate environment. I think we have come to believe that because we live in a land of opportunity, that anyone who is not prosperous and doing well only has themselves to blame. That any young person who wears a hood is a dangerous gangster. I think this is a dangerous position to be in, but a position that we are in because we take everything that is presented by the media about problems in our society at face value. Because the media more often than not presents the negative that is going on rather than the positive, because there is a view that this is what people are interested in. Even when issues are raised – perhaps so that something can be done about the situation – the meaning is at times lost in the sensationalised headlines.

So when I picked up a local newspaper and saw a headline, the worst 20 places to live in Milton Keynes with the caption "Netherfield takes over Beanhill," the immediate message is not that there are problems within these areas for which more needs to be done to understand and overcome the problems. Rather the immediate message that I received was that these are not places where you would want to live. Initially, I was put off reading the article by this message. When I finally did read it, it was not until I got to the end that I realised that a point being made was that more needed to be done. The problem, however, is I'm not sure how many people would read the whole article, but would simply, come to a conclusion on the basis of the headlines.

I would be happier if the heading read differently. The point, however, is that if I read or was told something negative about a friend or an acquaintance. I would not just accept what I heard at face value. I would start by questioning whether or not what I have been told is actually true. If I found it to be true, I would question the circumstances that led to the situation/actions that were taken. Even if the circumstances could in no way justify the actions that were taken, unless what was done was absolutely atrocious, I would not condemn the person as bad and think – tough as regard to anything that subsequently happened. The key thing is that there is a link between myself and such a person – I know them, I know something of the person's character, circumstances and background. With most of the people we read about, especially when reference is made to an individual or family in a neighbourhood, we don't know them and equally as important we don't know if they are really representative of the other people in their neighbourhood.

If we are solely reliant on media headlines for our understanding of our wider community, I believe that we are setting ourselves up to fail. We need to go a few steps further, to challenge and contain the power of media messages by enhancing our understanding.

If we begin to ask questions and try to understand the real stories behind the headlines, I believe this will take us a long way towards understanding what is really going on. The challenge will then be how to effectively utilise the insights that we have obtained.

Who are the People in Your Neighbourhood - Common Purpose

(Understanding the place where you live)

Oh, who are the people in your neighborhood?
In your neighborhood?
In your neighborhood?
Say, who are the people in your neighborhood?
The people that you meet each day
Seasame Street

I have a much more in-depth picture of my community now than I did a year ago. Fortunately for me, my learning was accelerated through the leadership programme – Common Purpose. Per chance I came across Common Purpose or, rather, it came across me. I registered and attended a networking event. Following on from this the Programme Director for Milton Keynes contacted me, asking if I wanted to meet up. At this point I was clueless as to what Common Purpose was about, but as there is a direct link between leadership training and human resources, I thought I'd take up the invitation as there may be an opportunity for collaboration. Though I had been provided with a bit of literature on Common Purpose, it did not really provide a clear picture of what it is all about, so I was pleasantly surprised when I met with Kate Davidson and she began to explain the programme to me.

Everyone who's been in a Common Purpose programme is likely to describe it differently. Common Purpose may be best positioned to describe itself, however, I refer to it as a street MBA that provides you with the opportunity to network with different leaders from the private, public and voluntary sector within your area. From this perspective, I've not only gained some good contacts, I've also made some very good friends. It has also afforded me the opportunity to become both a Countec Business Ambassador and Young Enterprise judge. More pertinently for me, it has also provided an insight into civil society. It affords you the opportunity to visit places and meet people from different parts of the community; from political leaders, business owners to everyday people, and gain an insight and understanding into the way in which things really work. I doubt if I would have ever been in a position to write this book if not for Common Purpose.

Although I had been in Milton Keynes for over 3 years when I went on the Common Purpose programme, it wasn't until then that I first visited Netherfield – a part of Milton Keynes that now has a very special place in my heart. It's also largely from a Common Purpose programme day that I had the first opportunity to gain some insight into the socio-economic issues of Milton Keynes and talk to people with direct involvement with a number of the projects and concerns within Milton Keynes. It also provided me with a direct inroad to developing a good network within Milton Keynes. So to me, Common Purpose is a very good starting point for gaining an insight into, and some understanding of, the place where you live.

I do, however, recognise that Common Purpose is not for everyone and the programmes do not exist in every town, so there must be other means that can be adopted to gain an insight into society. Perhaps there are other programmes out there that are worth enquiring about.

The key point is that while Common Purpose provided me with a quick route into the different aspects and spectrums of Milton Keynes, for me it was more than anything what whet my appetite. I didn't stop with the programme days, I started visiting places that I would not normally visit – even if it was just for a drive around an area. I started talking to people who are directly involved in the work across Milton Keynes. So for people who will not get involved with programmes like Common Purpose, I believe the key is to visit different projects and places and talk to people with some form of involvement in areas outside our normal sphere.

INFLUENCING AND PARTICIPATING WITH THE MEDIA

Sane and intelligent human beings are like all other human beings,
and carefully and cautiously and diligently conceal their private real
opinions from the world
and give out fictitious ones in their stead for general consumption.
MARK TWAIN

The many organisations that are directly involved in the community very rarely advertise what they do – at least not on a wide scale. The tendency is for them to communicate with their networks, which are often quite small. They also tend not to announce their successes. Subsequently, if you do not have a direct link to them, unless you have perchance just heard of them, it is unlikely that you will know who they are, what they do and what they have achieved. Most of us are aware of the large charitable organisations like the Red Cross and Childline, NSPCC, NSPCA due to their long-term existence and the scale of their operations. I'm aware that from time to time organisations such as Childline and World Vision will advertise on television. I can't however remember seeing a feature programme highlighting the work of such organisations. On the odd occasion when things are not quite working out in areas of London such as Brixton, I see people such as Camilla Batmanghelidjh of Kid's Company or Shaun Bailey (a well-known London youth worker) interviewed on television about the issues that lead to the problems on the street. Very rarely are they given the opportunity to explain the background issues, what they are doing to combat the issues, the successes they have had and how other people can help. I believe the same applies at a local level within Milton Keynes with local media.

I don't believe that the media is entirely responsible for this. If you talk to a good newspaper editor, I believe he or she would say that they are interested in publishing good stories. So if they are not informing the public enough of the positive things the first question to be asked is whether or not the media is aware of these stories. If not, is it because nobody has taken the time to tell the media – possibly because the people involved are too caught up trying to make things work or possibly have assumed that the media will not be interested? Or have the people involved perhaps tried to present these stories to the media, but received a negative response either because the story was not clearly presented or because truly it was not sensational enough? Whatever the case, I believe it is time for both the issues that lead to social problems and successes in overcoming them to start filtering through to the media – ultimately getting through to the public – in order to increase public awareness, increase involvement and improve public perceptions.

For this reason, when I heard the vision for Milton Keynes Television (MKTV) I was very much interested in doing what I could do, as an individual, to help make it work. I hoped other people would be interested in doing the same, as the vision of MKTV was for it to be a community television station for Milton Keynes, with a national presence.

I'd hoped that, with support, MKTV would have become an exemplary television station working together with Milton Keynes online television station (Ask MK), Radio station – Horizon and two local newspapers – *The Citizen* and *MK News* (and even the BBC Three Counties radio station) in order to provide an insight into what is going on in different areas of our community.

Although MKTV is no longer on the air and it may not be back, it's still amazing that we have so many tools at our disposal to use to increase awareness and really and truly benefit the whole community.

Have you ever been there? A Moment of Introspection

*How far you go in life depends on your being tender with the young,
compassionate with the aged,
sympathetic with the striving and tolerant of the weak and strong.
Because someday in life you will have been all of these.*
Geⱺrge Washington Carver

Over and over again I will say that people are predominantly the same, with the same basic hopes, desires and dreams. Over recent years, the middle class has blossomed and grown. The expanded middle class does not come from upper-class people, but people from a working class background who have been able to develop themselves through hard work or what have you to get to their current position.

Anyone in this position needs only to think back to what life used to be like – to the challenges they faced at home and in their neighbourhood – to gain some insight into the way people in this position today (or even worse off) must feel. The only thing is you need to multiply the pain, frustration etc. of how they must feel because today, unlike before, they are surrounded by an opulence which is highlighted and shoved in their faces by media focus.

Hopefully by now it is clear that not everyone is in this position simply because they want to be there and refuse to get off their behinds and do something.

Anyone who was ever young – and my guess is that that is everyone – will know what it is like to be young. Each person's youth will be somewhat different, but there are some features that I believe will be common to most people. There will be the challenges of growing up and maturing – being something between a child and an adult; the challenge of trying to establish an identity, working out what you want to do with your life, because somehow you knew that you had to do something; the realisation of what you wanted to do but not knowing how to get there; possibly not having the confidence to step out and just do it or having the people to provide you with the guidance to do it. Possibly you were fortunate – you were confident, you knew what you wanted and you had all the guidance, support and resources you needed to get there. Stop and imagine the difference it would make if one of those elements were missing.

Remember the silly things that you did when you were young (and possibly the things you still do)? Those things that you think of now and can't imagine for the life of you what got into your head. If you begin to think of all those things, then you may begin to understand why, in a world that is much more complex than ever before, young people behave in the way they do.

This does not undermine the fact that some of the things that young people do are questionable. I'd, however, really like to see us asking the question why, in order to understand their perspectives on things and support and guide them instead of condemning them

So when we think of people in different circumstances, the key is to try and put ourselves in their position and think of what we would need to help us in those circumstances. This is not, however, to say that we should just rush out and act. There is still a need to cross-check and make sure that our theories will work in practical terms for the people we have in mind.

Establishing solutions begins with hearing things from the perspective of the people facing the issues and understanding where they are coming from. I believe this gives people a sense of hope and confidence. I remember when I was growing up my biggest frustration was that I believed nobody cared or really understood me. Whenever a person would take the time to listen to me and understand things from my perspective. I became very open to their point of view. I felt motivated. I felt a greater sense of purpose and I excelled. While I now have much more self confidence, I am not really that much different today.

Past experience has, however, taught me to confront the situations and people that do things I find upsetting, and I can hardly count the number of times that I have confronted situations only to find that the other party did not quite mean things in the way I thought they did and have been rather surprised at my interpretation of the situation. Has this ever happened to you?

Get Out there or help someone else to do so - Volunteering and Sponsorship

Nothing brings me more happiness than trying to help the most
vulnerable people in society.
It is a goal and an essential part of my life - a kind of destiny.
Whoever is in distress can call on me.
I will come running wherever they are.
PRINCESS DIANA

I recently got a letter through my letterbox informing me that one of my neighbours, together with 23 other men and women, would be taking part in the Flora London Marathon. The 24 of them would be chained together throughout the race with the aim of beating the existing Guinness World Recordof 17. This is aimed at raising funds for a children's cancer charity. Now that I've mentioned it, I'd better remember to make a contribution. I doubt if I'll ever run a marathon myself, but I can always try and support those that do.

Possibly the most obvious thing to do to try and make a difference is to volunteer. It is something that numerous people already do in so many different ways. With around 1400 voluntary organisations with a base in Milton Keynes there cannot be a shortage of opportunities. In fact, I've heard that approximately one in every two people in Milton Keynes volunteers in some capacity. The fact that we already have so many volunteers could lead to the conclusion that we already have enough volunteers and don't require any more. This is not, however, true as whenever I speak to a voluntary organisation two of the greatest challenges they say they face are the need for more funding and volunteers. Voluntary organisations are always looking for volunteers, be it to help with frontline services, business support, fund-raising, ambassadors or what have you. But if you ask, there will always be a way in which they could use some support.

I've already suggested that there should be more joint working between voluntary organisations. I would also like to now raise the question as to whether or not they are getting enough support in the key areas to make a fundamental difference.

I must confess that when the social problems that we face were first highlighted to me, I wanted to rush out and set up an organisation to do things to make a difference. Taking cognisance of what is already in place I had to stop myself and think of how I could best add additional value to what is already in place.

With so many things out there, possibly this is a key concern that holds numerous people back. What can I do? Where can I volunteer? Unfortunately, it is not easy to gain access to information on the different opportunities that exist. I do, however, believe that a good starting point lies with what you are good at. I think a second critical question to ask is where is there the most need – in general terms and specifically for the things that you are good at, enjoy doing and/or are passionate about.

For a number of people, however, the biggest restraint from volunteering is time. I can talk about how little time is really needed to volunteer and sometimes all that is required is a little creativity to allocate some time, but for some people it is not going to make the difference as some people really and truly just don't have the time. There are still numerous other things that can be done.

You can't talk about volunteering without going on to talk about sponsorship. Since the days of Live Aid, there has been an ever-growing spotlight on the problems of Africa and the rest of the developing world. People have responded in different ways - critically, they have volunteered, they have provided general donations and they have sponsored programmes or children. I believe the focus here has been further enhanced by the trend towards Corporate Social Responsibility. I think these are good things and I have no desire to detract from this, but how about our Corporate Social Responsibility at home?

An Orchestra of Agencies

Harmony makes small things grow,
Lack of it makes great things decay
SALLUST QUOTE

I'm amazed at the number of agencies that exist in Milton Keynes, especially as there must be a lot of overlap in what they do and the geographical areas that they cover. Beyond a shadow of a doubt they all have good intentions, but logic says that they cannot all be working effectively if they end up duplicating each other.

With the wide number I do, however, feel that they have had a rather limited impact on some of the areas they work in. I'm not one hundred percent sure of the reason for this. It could be something to do with the fact that a number of them cover similar areas and possibly there is a lot of overlap and duplication. It could be that while they are working very hard, they are not actually covering the areas where there is the greatest need as they don't have a grasp on the real issues; they are doing what government – possibly central government requires, but not what the people really want or need – on the basis of my understand at times it feels to me as if the Government does more fire-fighting and focuses a lot more on symptoms than on the root causes.

I understand that the key challenges for voluntary organisations is funding. It is limited and usually only provided to agencies for a short fixed period of time ranging from one to five years, which is often not much time to achieve the required results, especially within a very competitive environment. The truth is that the world as a whole is becoming increasingly competitive – I think competition is engrained in human nature. There is possibly no arena that is more competitive than the business world and I think there are lessons for any voluntary organisation that truly wants to be effective within the business sector.

Privately owned organisations compete, however, there is an increased amount of collaboration between them as well. Taking things a step further – the mergers and acquisitions market is booming. Could voluntary organisations possibly do more of what they are trying to achieve if they were more collaborative? After all, the most important thing should be the end result. When Childline was threatened due to a lack of funding, it was taken over by the NSPCC, ensuring that both the services of the NSPCC and Childline which both share the same vision for children and had a history of working together, continued, to the benefit of the young people they serve.

Don't get me wrong, I am aware that some agencies do work in conjunction with each other – at the very least on a referral basis. This is illustrated by a homeless man I spoke to who found that once he got support from the first agency, he was continually referred on to other agencies for other areas of support, and I could see how this referred support could actually help him all the way until he gets back on his feet again. I recognise that it is easy to comment from the outside, but to be honest with the best of efforts; I don't believe this always happens and I believe that much more can be done. So as the voluntary organisations and other agencies continue the good work that they are doing - hopefully working closely together, I hope the rest of us continually find new ways to support their work.

CREDIT UNION

Lack of money is the root of all evil.
GEORGE BERNARD SHAW

I recently went to Stantonbury Campus, where one of the collection points for Milton Keynes Credit Union is based. You see, in Milton Keynes there are a number of people who do not have bank accounts. I can't say whether or not they all want bank accounts, but it's fair to say that unfortunately, it's not easy for everyone to open a bank account or get a loan. I don't fully understand why, but I believe it is fair to say it relates to the banking regulations, credit rating and the banks' perception of the level of risk that they may be exposed to by providing people with their services. Unfortunately the people most often denied access to the banking system are the people most in need and with very few alternatives. I believe the intentions are good, but unfortunately, if someone is in desperate need, they are going to need to access funds somehow. Yes, the ideal is that people don't get into situations that place them in a position of need. The reality, however, is that from time to time most of us get into this type of situation. For those of us that have full access to the financial structures in place, we are provided with the means to pick ourselves up and continue. For those that don't, the options seem to be to stay where we are, sink, or rely on negative means to get up and pull ourselves up – hopefully on a temporary basis, but sadly at times on a long-term basis – unless we have some ingenuity or near miraculous means of getting out of the situation.

By negative means I mean vice, or falling into the hands of loan sharks, which may ultimately lead to vice. By ingenuity, perhaps we discover that we have an entrepreneurial spirit that provides us with thoughts or ideas that help us to get up and continue. By miraculous means, I mean that there is some kind person who offers help or a structured organisation set up to provide advice and support – an organisation such as a credit union.

Fortunately, Milton Keynes recently started a credit union with both savings and loan facilities. Currently it has collection points at Bletchley, Stantonbury and Wolverton. Hopefully over time they will have a broadened range of services with collection points across the city. They are currently in the process of recruiting a Development Officer who I believe will help with this. The only thing is that they still need people to get involved. They need people to volunteer. However, not everyone can do this, because of the time involved. I believe virtually everyone can, however, open an account with their local credit union and there is really nothing to lose by doing so – in fact there is possibly a lot more to gain than just the knowledge that someone else might be helped by your funds – as somewhere along the line, if you have a need for a low-interest loan, you will be perfectly positioned to get one.

To me, this is a no-brainer. I'm not sure how much of a difference they will make; it's early days yet for our credit union in Milton Keynes, but I believe I've nothing to lose. It's just like the fact that while I don't play the lottery, I do own bonds. I've only earned a few hundred pounds through them as compared to the millions I might have won through the lottery. I do, however, still have my initial capital intact. So I went to Stantonbury Campus and opened a credit union account. I might not gain large returns from it and I haven't put all my savings in, but I have put something in and I believe it will go some way to making a difference.

Our Heritage

History will be kind to me
For I intend to write it.
Sir Winston Churchill

Milton Keynes has been designed with a centre which is a focal point. The civic offices are in Central Milton Keynes as is the theatre district with the clubs, the shopping centre, the Xscape building with the ski dome, and many (though not all) of the large offices amongst other things. It was purposely designed this way and I have nothing against this; the only thing is with the design and concentration around the Centre for new people coming into Milton Keynes we often forget the original three towns of Milton Keynes – Bletchley, Stony Stratford and Wolverton – which all have their unique characteristics with things to offer, which I hope we do not neglect.

Bletchley was the largest of the three towns. It is in fact home to many industries. Last year it became home to Asda and IKEA, which has led to more people visiting the area. It is also now home to the new football stadium for the Milton Keynes Dons, which will no doubt help to put Bletchley back in the focus of our minds and on the map. Possibly more significant, if not more important, however, is Bletchley Park, which is something we should really be shouting about. As mentioned earlier the German codes were broken in Bletchley during World War II – so in effect Milton Keynes helped to save the war. For Bletchley Park to continue to stand, it does, however, need investment for its sustainability.

Then we have Stony Stratford. To an extent I believe Stony Stratford has done a good job of retaining its original unique identity. The first time I visited Stony was at Christmas. I drove through the high street, alight with all its Christmas decorations, and all the different shops and thought that it was a place that I must definitely come back to explore. I know that there are a lot of high streets but there is something different about Stony. You've got to visit to really understand what I mean about this charming little town.

I'd been to Wolverton a few times to see a friend but it wasn't until I went to visit some friends and saw all the children out playing in the fields behind their house that I truly appreciated the beauty and the spirit of Wolverton. However in my mind, Wolverton has possibly lost out quite a lot with the development of the new town. I wouldn't necessarily say that Wolverton's current position is solely down to the presence and development of Milton Keynes as a Centre. As mentioned previously Wolverton was, however, home to Wolverton Works railway repair depot and Mcclaughin printers. It also had what was then a major railway. Though in time Wolverton Works and Mcclaughin's may have ceased to exist, there is a sense that with the development of Milton Keynes and the centralisation of everything - Wolverton was left with nothing. It's nice that Wolverton is home to Milton Keynes' museum. It would be great to see something put in Wolverton that highlights its significance in the history of Milton Keynes and for its future.

CREATIVE ARTS

A sincere artist is not one who makes a faithful attempt to put on to canvas what is in front of him,
but one who tries to create something which is, in itself, a living thing.
WILLIAM DOBELL

I'm big on the creative arts, I always have been - be it music, theatre, artwork, poetry, prose, you name it - any form of creative expression. Possibly this stems from the fact that in the times in my life when I have felt low and unable to talk to someone who I believe will understand, I have used poetry to express the way I feel or at times I've lost myself in music. As a result I have learnt to both appreciate not just the beauty but, more pertinently, the power of creative arts.

The creative arts are well represented in Milton Keynes, supported by the presence of organisations such as Kik Music, the Youth Music Project; MK City Orchestra, Osagyefo Theatre company – an African Dance & Music Project, Wolverton City Garden Society, and a number of independent artists to mention a few.

The project which has stood out for me and really got me excited is the banners and underpass project - On the Verge Gateway Project, which is being led by a local artist who has the dream of drawing people from local communities through the use of art, refurbishing and using artwork to draw people from different communities together. Involving both young and old people alike and helping them to develop new schools.

The biggest frustration is that she struggled for years to get the sponsorship and support to make it happen. When I first heard the artist, Myriam, speak, it would have been easy to walk away on the basis that it is a great idea that will naturally happen. Indeed because of her dedication and hard work, it deserves to happen. In fact it has now started to happen. If you go to Oldbrook, Fishermead, Bradwell Common and Conniburrow you will see some beautiful banners that have been created by local artists based on ideas inspired by work with local residents. This is great! It is, however, just the start. It's going to need a lot more support to reach its full potential so I hope people find out more about it, share in the vision, and get involved to enable it to develop to its full potential.

Do It Yourself – Lakes Youth

*"Man's mind, once stretched by a new idea,
never regains its original dimensions."*
OLIVER WENDELL HOLMES

In 2006 a young man named Ray Quinn appeared in the talent show The X Factor. I couldn't help but like him. While he remained true to who he was he was extremely grateful for the opportunity of being on the show and wanted to make people, especially his mentor, Simon Cowell, proud. He went on to the finals and finished as the runner-up. In 2007, I felt proud to see him judging on Baby Ballroom, another talent contest.

In some many ways, he reminds me of some other young people I know of in Milton Keynes who live on the Lakes Estate. I guess like most young people they were of the opinion that they never had enough to do - they were bored. On the Lakes Estate there is an officer called a Community Mobiliser who has responsibility for community development within the area.

Described by a local parent as "someone who gets things going or keeps things going in the community.", recognising the frustrations of the young people, the community mobiliser worked with them to arrange a number of sporting events. This included the rare opportunity to go away for an event outside of the estate and as such broaden their horizons. To her credit the events were a great success. They both involved and effectively engaged a lot of the young people. Significantly, they have carried on since the first event. What stands out about the events now is that they are no longer organised by the Community Mobiliser. Rather they are actually organised by the young people themselves. The only thing that the Community Mobiliser does to help is provide them with support at their request.

Their activities have had such an impact that they received the Queen's Award for Voluntary Services in 2005. And some of these boys, though still quite young now are very conscious of their community needs and are working to help fulfil the needs of the young children on the estate who look up to them. They also work to support the older people within their community. To this end some of these young people also go to meetings within the Council Offices to represent their community's needs.

It's amazing how little things have such a huge impact. After all, these are young people that the typical adult would not think of talking to, who on their own part were very shy and would not have even contemplated conversing with adults, who now go to meetings and clearly articulate their viewpoint on behalf of the whole of their community.

There are a total of eight community mobilisers in Milton Keynes, working across the most deprived areas. Taking the time to understand the community needs and support the communities in fulfilling them through a number of different means inclusive of activity groups, workshops, trips and outings, but ultimately providing local people who sincerely care about their communities with the opportunity to improve on things for the collective good.

On YouTube there are a few videos which much better highlight the work of Community Mobilisers than I ever could. [15]

Foot Soldiers

I am the Unknown Soldier
And maybe I died in vain
But if I were alive and my country called,
I'd do it all over again.
BILLY ROSE. AMERICAN THEATRICAL ENTREPRENEUR AND COMPOSER 1899-1966

In March 2007 I took up the invitation to attend an event organised by Milton Keynes Economy and Learning Partnership which was aimed at celebrating some of the work by different agencies within Milton Keynes. I had an awareness of and respect for the work of a number of the groups represented such as Countec, the Community Mobilisers, and Kik Music. There was, however, also present an organisation called NEET Outreach, whose work I was unaware of. I therefore spent a significant amount of time talking to one of the workers in order to learn more about their work. Though NEET had only two employees, it is an organisation of what I would refer to as foot soldiers.

NEET, standing for Not in Education, Employment or Training, had the objective of identifying and making contact with young people who are NEET and supporting them to become EET – In Education, Employment or Training.

I believe that there are a number of organisations that work with one or the other if not all of these categories of young people for a period of time. The key differences with the NEET project is that while with most organisations the young people had to go to the organisations, with NEET the Outreach Workers went out on foot to identify the young people, build relationships with them and provide them with the long-term support, guidance and support they needed.

Critically NEET provided young people with both the skills development and employment support that enable young people to prioritise their goals and meet their individual needs.

Within a short period of the year for which NEET was funded, it was able to get set up and build relevant relationships with other agencies, which enabled it to go on to impact the lives of around 100 young people to some degree. By working with different agencies across the city, NEET was able to help 23 people into employment and 67 with their skills development.[16]

I'm conscious that NEET adopted a time-consuming process which cannot be emulated by all agencies. However, I believe they reached young people that others were unable to reach – possibly some of the people that were at most risk of falling into a lifelong gap and therefore are some of the young people that most needed help and support. It's quite sad that NEET received funding for only one year.

Business Involvement – Rok – The Nation's Local Builder

*"Social obligation is much bigger than supporting worthy causes.
It includes anything that impacts people and the quality of their lives."*
William Ford Jr., Chairman, Ford Motor Co.

There is currently a big buzz within business around corporate social responsibility (CSR) and you will increasingly find a section on company websites entitled Corporate Social Responsibility outlining how the company works to meet its social responsibility.

In many ways I believe Rok, aptly sloganed "The nation's local builder", have got it right. Not perfect but right. As their name suggests, Rok is a national building firm. While being national, they aim to be an integral part of the local communities in the areas that they are based in.

I first took notice of Rok when I started hearing people mention the artwork done on an underpass at the Lake estate which was project-managed by Rok. A couple of different people that I spoke to cited the underpass as something that had been done and gone a long way to foster community relationships.

Subsequently I was in a conversation with Rok's Milton Keynes Area Manager when he naturally and promptly and without hesitation expressed interest in supporting another community project. This led me to arrange a meeting to gain a further understanding of Rok, what they do, and why.

When I met with Mike he explained that Rok was built on the basis of the good old England that we often reminisce about. Rok's vision is to be the trusted neighbourhood builder at the end of the street and as such an integral part of the community. The fulfilment of this vision is aided by the fact that most of its employees live locally.

To this end each year each area office aims at getting involved in two main projects - a charity project and a community project. On a charity the staff go out into the local community and work on an identified project. Community day is more focused on skills transfer as this is a project that is project-managed by Rok.

While Rok's employees are encouraged to identify projects where the organisation can provide support, Rok recognises that they will not always be best placed to identify areas where they can most effectively provide input. Critically Rok therefore maintains contact with organisations such as MKCVO and Milton Keynes Community Foundation in order to obtain information on areas of need in order to make informed decisions on where there is a need for which their skills can best be used.

If I doubted for one minute the integrity of what I was told by Rok's management any doubts were allayed when I bumped into an old friend who had recently started working with Rok. I got into a conversation with him about work. I was amazed to find that, unprompted, he repeated a lot of what the Area Manager had said when I spoke to him, sharing the business ethos with me in a manner that indicated that he truly believed in it.

It's difficult for me to say what other organisations are doing – or not doing – with regard to corporate social responsibility, but without a doubt I believe that Rok is definitely doing something right, not only as regards the local community but critically also with its employees. So much so, that when I recently bumped into someone who was looking for support from organisations on a project and I mentioned Rok, he responded that he was looking for an organisation that is not already involved in the community.

As a result, may I hold out the baton to you? Will you run with it?

One Step Further – Long-Term Involvement

*"People glorify all sorts of bravery
except the bravery they might show on behalf of their nearest
neighbors."*
George Eliot Middlemarch

On the basis of what I have heard both from Rok and also unsolicited from other people, I believe that Rok is doing a great job. I don't believe they are the only organisation that is taking a step to impact on communities, but I do believe that they have a model which is to be emulated.

I would, however, like to see the increased development of modules that foster long-term relationships to the mutual benefit of both communities and businesses.

Organisations such as Rok go a long way to impact on local communities. The only question is whether they are missing a trick – could they possibly go a step or two further for the mutual benefit of both individuals within the community and the future of their businesses?

There are a number of young people who have never been beyond the local area in which they live and have definitely never been into an office. So what if following on from a community project, young people were invited for a tour of the organisation's office to gain a clearer understanding of where they work and what they do? This would help to broaden the horizon of some of the young people (and it does not have to be exclusively young people). This would also give the organisation the opportunity to showcase their business if not to potential recruits, to people likely to at least go away and speak highly of the organisation. There are so many options available today, but most people lack an understanding of what they are or how to access them. It does not have to be a large group of people; even doing this with two or three people could make a difference.

If organisations believe that this is something that they are unable to do, then it would be nice to know that employees involved within the projects were perhaps encouraged to mentor people they work with, support or provide guidance on future projects/project enhancements. After all, a link has been created. It would be sad to see it go to waste.

FIVE A DAY AT THE LAKES

An apple a day keeps the doctor away
Apple in the morning - Doctor's warning
Roast apple at night - starves the doctor outright
Eat an apple going to bed - knock the doctor on the head
Three each day, seven days a week - ruddy apple, ruddy cheek
OLD NURSERY RHYME

By now you would expect that every citizen in Milton Keynes and the UK as a whole would be eating a healthy diet with the recommended five fruits and vegetables a day as, over recent years, there has been an increasing amount of talk about the need for healthy living. It has now permeated the ethos of most corporate organisations as they started off by talking about work-life balance and have now gone on to talk about health and wellbeing with the objective of promoting all forms of healthy living for employees.

It doesn't stop with organisations. The government is promoting healthy living too. There is a lot of talk about healthy eating and the government is actively promoting it within schools, providing schools with guidelines about the type of food that should be provided. There are adverts on telly promoting healthy eating. And lauding the benefits of eating five a day. The major supermarkets have started labelling foods to indicate how much of your five a day you will gain from consuming a product.

You would therefore expect everyone to have got the message by now, to understand the consequences of not eating their five a day, the benefits of doing so, and to have responded accordingly. It is not however, happening. For some people they may be taking on a bloody-minded attitude which means that they simply refuse to because they don't want to be dictated to by government or anyone else for that matter, besides, they like their current diet.

You could easily assume that if it is reported that the people of the Lakes Estate aren't eating their five a day, it is for such reasons. The truth, however, is whether or not they want to respond, even when you put the cost of fruits and vegetables aside, there is still a key limitation. There is no shop that sells fresh fruits and vegetables within the Lakes Estate and the Lakes Estate is somewhat isolated from other places including the nearest Sainsbury's, Tesco or Asda, which are in Bletchley. Sainsbury's is the closest major supermarket and almost two miles away. A lot of the people on the estate do not have cars, and it is an established fact that our transport system in Milton Keynes is our greatest weakness.

So I ask the question: in a world where we are constantly talking about corporate social responsibility, wouldn't it be nice if Tesco, Sainsbury's, Asda or any other supermarket chain built a little local store in the Lakes Estate? I'm sure they would gain a lot of support in obtaining the land or building to do so. We often hear of them building Tesco stores where the local people don't want them. This is a place where the people want and would truly appreciate it, and I believe it would be a great way of demonstrating corporate social responsibility which would have a long-term impact which is well within the means of such an organisation.

Leave Your Car at Home

I love the Redways and at times I use them for short walks, particularly when I'm going for the short walk from my home in Medbourne to Hazeley. In our green-conscious environment it would be criminal to drive (except possibly for reasons such as rain or darkness).

As much as I love them and use them I am, however, conscious that they are not as well utilised as you would have hoped. Typical reasons cited for the under utilisation of the redways are the fact that the greenery is quite high, hiding the paths from the road – you may see this is the original purpose. This does however create a security concern for the few people that do use them.

Personally, I believe this concern would be minimised if not totally eliminated if they were much better utilised.

At the same time, public transport in Milton Keynes is limited. But it is said that the use of public transport has increased – possibly because more recent growth in Milton Keynes has included a number of people who are reliant on public transport. As much as the number of users has increased, it has not increased to the extent that the quality of services in terms of frequency of buses has sufficiently increased. I don't believe this will happen until there is a significant increase in the number of users.

Taking these two points in mind, I'd love Milton Keynes to conduct an experiment. Let's have a "Leave your car at home" week. Not by compulsion, but by choice. Having said this, I must confess that while I recycle and try not to be wasteful I'm not a green party member who believes that everyone should give up their cars – I don't believe it's a practical option. However the period that I suggest is simply a week which would hopefully develop into an annual event where everyone was encouraged to leave their cars at home for a week or even just a day – walking, cycling or getting the bus (or train) to their destinations. If it helps, we could use the environmental greenness buses to promote it.

The thinking behind this is that if a high number of people use the redways at this point in time it will encourage them to use them going forward. If we have an improved bus service for a week which everyone is encouraged to use, then perhaps more people will see the benefits of using buses and see them as a possible option, start using them more and as a result allow for more frequent buses to be available for all to use.

Food Banks

Little deeds of kindness,
little words of love,
make our earth an Eden,
like the heaven above.
Little Drops of Water by Julia Carney, 1845

Most people have at some point in time gone through one or two tough patches – be it that they last for weeks, months or sadly even years. For some people the worst of a tough patch may mean the need to cut back on expenses. For others it may mean that people struggle to pay bills and even to put food on the table.

Fortunately for people in Milton Keynes that are faced with such situations there are two food banks that I am aware of that aim to support people during these times.

There is one based at St Mary's Church through which they work along with a number of other local churches collect food contributions which are then delivered to people in need.

They work in conjunction with the other food bank, which is based at Milton Keynes Christian Centre, and is registered as an independent charity which works with different agencies across Milton Keynes to support people in need.

Milton Keynes Food Bank operates on a voucher/referral system whereby people who visit a number of different agencies within the City and are identified as people with highlighted needs, inclusive of those provided for by the Food Bank, are provided with vouchers which enable them to go to the food bank to obtain a free food parcel.

Food for the food banks comes from local community and church congregation members who make donations of tinned and dried food or finance (for the purchase of food). One of the great things is that the people who donate include people who may have benefited from the food banks in the past, such as a lady who benefited from a food bank during a tough period when she had a small baby. Recognising that the food bank did not store baby food, she made a decision to donate baby food. In addition there are a number of organisations (both within and outside of Milton Keynes) such as New Covent Garden Food which also donate to the food bank.

When I learnt about the food bank, I made a decision to make a monthly contribution to it. Specifically I give myself a monthly budget which has changed over time from £5.00 to either £10 or £20 dependant on my budget for the month. (The change in amount is aimed at covering rises in the cost of living). In the grand scheme of things it's not a significant amount of money for me; I often spend that amount or more on a night out. But that's not the point.

On my designated food bank weekend, I go to the shops with my shopping budget, normally in cash as to meet my objectives, it is important that I keep within my budget. The task is to buy something reasonable within my budget for a family, couple or individual, ensuring that I only buy for them things that I would buy myself. Subsequently, as I don't generally buy economy products for myself, I don't buy them for anyone else. I generally find it challenging to walk out of the shop with something reasonable within my budget, but I make it a point to stick within my budget, because I want to put myself in that position so that I have a greater understanding and empathy for the people I'm helping.

At times like Christmas, I often leave the shops feeling quite sad. For some reason (maybe it's my imagination,) things seem to be more expensive at Christmas, but there are still an overwhelming number of people walking around filling their trolleys until they nearly overflow as I carry a little basket, trying to pick up a few things that are actually affordable. I often wonder whether they will ever be able to eat all that food over the Christmas period and question what Christmas is now about. But this is not the point either.

The point is that for someone on a limited budget, such as people on benefits or facing a temporary setback, it must be hard. Income support does not allow for much more in a week than what I budget to contribute to the food banks. For this reason amongst others I very much doubt that there are many people that live off of benefits unless they feel - rightly or wrongly, that they are compelled to do so. Don't get me wrong, I know that there are people who are out to play the system, but for the vast majority of people on benefits, it is not by choice.

A Bit of Extracare

I have enjoyed greatly the second blooming...
suddenly you find - at the age of 50, say
- that a whole new life has opened before you.
AGATHA CHRISTIE

With the current concerns about the provisions for older citizens, it's nice to know that there are a number of provisions in Milton Keynes for them, as though we do have a relatively young population, we also have a number of older citizens, especially a number of the original residents and earlier arrivals into the new town.

The provisions for older citizens are varied. Some may choose to stay in their own homes and be comfortable and are able to do so, whilst others may move in within family members. Outside of this there is a variety of housing schemes available. One that I have an opportunity to visit, that therefore stands out to me is Extracare Charitable Trust's retirement village, Lovat Village, which opened in 2007 with almost 260 apartments and bungalows. I believe Lovat village is quite special because, whilst residents can live totally independently within the village, coming and going as and when they please, they also interact freely with other residents, either on a one-to-one basis or within groups. Lovat Village is a very lively place, buzzing with activities, both those arranged and taking place internally and those taking place outside of the village. I think it is worth making a visit to see.

If I'm still in Milton Keynes in my twilight years I'd certainly consider moving to Lovat Village or a similar home. However to keep such schemes running there is a need for community support. Indeed wherever our older residents live within our community, it is important that they are given all the support necessary. Extracare is a good start to this and they are doing a fantastic job, not only of making provisions, but also of creating awareness and engaging the community. When I talk to the staff at ExtraCare, it is, however, clear that they could always use a lot more support.

Social Capitalism

"The economics of the future is somewhat different.
You see, money doesn't exist in the 24th century...
The acquisition of wealth is no longer the driving force in our lives.
We work to better ourselves and the rest of humanity."
Jean-Luc Picard

The world experience of different political systems would indicate that, with all its imperfections and flaws, capitalism is the most accepted, if not the most effective, political system. Everything else does not seem to have worked properly - at least by the standards of the West. It is debatable as to whether or not the more autocratic systems of parts of the Middle East are successful or not. The truth, however, is that even if they are deemed a success in the Middle East they would never work in Western society more than any other reason for the simple fact that it would never be accepted. The fall of the Soviet Union signalled the end of Communism. When we talk of Socialism, I think of Animal Farm - all animals are equal, but some are more equal than others.

So we live in a capitalist society and the probability is that we always will. I don't personally believe that that is a bad thing. I myself happen to be a capitalist. I believe that people should be rewarded for their efforts and contributions to society. I must say that at times the concept seems a bit extreme - specifically when footballers are paid millions for playing ball. I guess this is tantamount to the value we place in what they do; otherwise hopefully this will one day correct itself.

More pertinently I detest the other extreme, when within the same environment there are people left in (relative) abject poverty. This has to be wrong. It's why I'm conscious that there are those that will always take advantage - I'm an advocate of a welfare system. Only I would love to see a welfare system that helped people up as opposed to the current system that, with all its complexities, often seems to hold people down.

As such whenever people have asked me about my political affiliation, I have responded that I am social capitalist. I expand that I advocate for social capitalism, a capitalism that is tempered with humanity that rewards people for their efforts, but never leaves people destitute in a manner that creates the increasingly polarised society that we seem to be developing today.

Social Capitalism is not so much about the haves being taxed for the sake of the have-nots. More pertinently, it's about people that have being conscious of those that have not and helping to support them as best as they can.

It's about the person living by himself in a four-bedroom house, but only using two of the rooms, recognising that someone else within the community is in desperate need of a roof over their head and providing him/her with a temporary shelter. In saying this, I am at the same time conscious that special care needs to be taken in taking such an action. There are, however, the more simple things such as giving the spare computer or television to someone who does not have one, rather than storing it in the garage or some other form of storage for the next five years. Taking some food to the food bank or to the person down the road who we know is going through a difficult patch. The truth is we usually have more than we need in our cupboards. Giving someone who would otherwise have none, one Christmas present and one each for our children instead of giving each of our children ten each. Importantly, these are decisions that people make of their own free will to give out of their excesses and, on occasion, even give sacrificially.

So to me social capitalism is not in the hands of the Government, but in the hands of a people who work hard for the security, wants and needs of themselves and their families, and are rewarded for doing so. But at the same time recognising that they can only consume so much and can take nothing to the grave and therefore take pleasure in supporting others too.

Landlord Responsibility

"The true measure of a man
is how he treats someone
who can do him absolutely no good."
Ann Landers

In 2006, there was a call by a number of local residents for the Council to provide Council accommodation for local residents. This is contrary to the direction in which England has been moving since the 1980s, but if nothing else it highlights that there is a problem with housing provision.

Though most people aspire to own their own home, even "affordable" social housing is not an (immediate) practical option for everyone. There will always be a significant proportion of the population that rents.

Although social housing (which is often offered on a shared ownership basis) is aimed at providing affordable accommodation for people who would not have otherwise been able to afford their own homes, there is still a question as to how affordable, affordable accommodation is, especially for people on lower incomes or only slightly above the minimum wage. For such people, rental accommodation is likely to be the only option available. With the shortage of Council accommodation people are increasingly reliant on renting from private landlords. To some extent it shouldn't really make much difference as to whether people rent from a private landlord, a social provider or a council. If anything, in many ways people should actually be in a better position if they rent from a private landlord. Unfortunately, this is not always the case.

While property is a good investment, renting property to people is the provision of a service which is equally (if not more) important. Unfortunately a lot of private landlords seem to be more focused on their investment with the objective of renting out properties for the highest return without a real focus on quality or the implications of their actions to both the tenants and the local area.

Not all landlords are guilty, I know a few that reference tenants and provide them with contracts which stipulate proper care, get involved in the local area and even attend local meetings. Sadly, there are a number of landlords who don't do any due diligence or take proper care. Take for instance the landlord of a friend of mine.

She lives in a five-bedroomed house at the end of a close, which was converted into a multi-occupancy home. I don't know if permission was sought for this, but if it was given, I think it was a mistake. Five rooms means five residents and often five cars – more when the tenants have visitors. This often causes problems between the tenants and other local residents. It's not what they bought into, but on the other hand it's where tenants live. My friend has found that over time, fellow tenants have moved in and out of the house; some get on well together, some don't, and at times when they don't there are quarrels or even fights that make her feel very uncomfortable.

For the local residents within her area, the positive thing is that this is the only multi-occupancy home on the close. Many have several which, when poorly managed, is problematic both for the tenants and other local residents.

Whether rental properties are based within established communities where existing housing stock is rented out or communities to be established as with new build properties (which are quite popular with landlords), there is a need for landlords to do due diligence, consider the implications of their setup on the area and take proper responsibility.

An Urban Eden

What matters is not necessarily the size of the dog in the fight
It's the size of the fight in the dog.
DWIGHT D. EISENHOWER

Have you heard of the campaign group Urban Eden? You see for many of us here Milton Keynes is our very own little Eden – in an urban area. That was the original plan for Milton Keynes and I believe that is what it is: undeniably urban, but at the same time very green.

The only problem is as we press on with the development of Milton Keynes there are concerns that some of the new plans may take away some of the things that make it the unique place that we love. It is recognised that some change is necessary for the growth and development of the city, but some of the proposals and plans just don't seem right to both the layman and to some of the professionals who were involved in the original planning. I guess it's all the more frustrating when some of the decisions seem to be made undemocratically with very little consultation.

To ensure that the concerns of the people are heard, expressed and responded to, Urban Eden has been set up. I find that increasingly when I talk to people who have read the views and concerns expressed by Urban Eden in the press they tend to agree with them. This informs me that Urban Eden has an important place in Milton Keynes even if, due to the level of frustration felt by members, the message may be delivered in what may be perceived as a confrontational manner (which may actually lead a number of additional people to hold back from getting involved). It does not, however, take away the fact that with hundreds of members who all want the best for city involved in Urban Eden, they do actively represent some of the needs of the people of Milton Keynes.

They do, however, only represent some of the needs, so it's good to hear that there will soon be a citizen's group in Milton Keynes which will bring together people from all areas of the community with the view to listen to and understand the issues and concerns of the people; to prioritise their needs and work together to find ways of making sure that the people's power is effectively used to resolve the issues.

My hope is that that while retaining its own unique identity, Urban Eden will soon be working with the citizen's group to ensure that the needs of all the people across the city are represented and heard.

Supporting those offering Support

I resolved to stop accumulating
and begin the infinitely more serious
and difficult task of wise distribution.
Surplus wealth is a sacred trust
which its possessor is bound to administer
in his lifetime for the good of the community.
Andrew Carnegie

When people identify an issue or area of concern, the response is often to go out and set up a new project or charity to deal with the issues; going straight out into an area of concern with all the best of intentions, but without doing any initial background research or at times to feel completely overwhelmed and unable to do anything to make a difference.

However, a new project/charity may very well be replicating things that already exist. Sometimes offering help without really understanding the environment may lead to a rejection, and doing nothing really doesn't make a difference. I've highlighted a few areas where I know that there are things going on, but to be honest my knowledge is somewhat limited.

I have, however, found the Milton Keynes Centre for Voluntary Organisations (MKCVO) to have a wealth of knowledge and information on what is going on: who is doing what, and where help is most needed. This is specifically relevant to people or organisations that want to provide direct support to projects.

A new scheme in Milton Keynes is the Charity Card, set up by Charity People. In addition to helping charities with their fundraising, Charity People offers a charity card to participating local charities. This enables businesses to support charities by providing products and services at discounted rates.

Finally for individuals and organisations that don't have the time or inclination to get directly involved and do not want to have to research the best projects to support financially, there is Milton Keynes Community Foundation which is a local, independent grant-making charity. Charities within the community can apply to the Foundation for grants, which are formally assessed by the Foundation which provides grants to the most appropriate projects based on donations made by individuals or organisations who may also choose to specify which charity their donations should go to.

Mind the Gaps 1 - Increasing the Viable Options of Future Generations

For nothing is fixed, forever and forever and forever, it is not fixed; the earth is always shifting, the light is always changing, the sea does not cease to grind down rock. Generations do not cease to be born, and we are responsible to them because we are the only witnesses they have. The sea rises, the light fails, lovers cling to each other, and children cling to us. The moment we cease to hold each other, the sea engulfs us and the light goes out.
James Baldwin

I wonder what the future holds for our young people. On a national, even global basis, but most specifically locally here in Milton Keynes. These days people - especially professionals – seem to work to live and not live to work. The worst thing is that we seem to think we actually have no choice and tend to give our children the message that they must do the same if they want a half-decent living. I wonder whether this is what we really want for our children. Even if it is, the question still remains as to whether it is the lifestyle that our children want for themselves.

If they don't – and there are indications that a number of them want a different lifestyle – as things currently stand, it might be quite difficult for them to have a descent standard of living without doing something that I would consider to be drastic, such as go into crime or be extremely "fortunate" enough to become a celebrity.

Contrary to popular belief, most of the young people I have spoken to are not interested in becoming celebrities (or in going into crime). The fact that a lot of boys wear saggy trousers and hoods does not mean that they are into crime, while, though young girls may be interested in dressing up and wearing makeup, it doesn't mean they are all obsessed by the celebrity culture.

Most young people just seem to want to hang out with friends, get a decent job that they enjoy, and eventually find someone to love who will love them in return; someone with whom they can set up a home and have kids with who they can shower with love. It usually really is that simple.

Some are easily influenced by others; many (just like you and I) make mistakes on the journey. Most would appreciate a little support and guidance; none want to be told what to do. I guess I've said it all before, but I feel the need to repeat it as I'm concerned that if we don't begin to break down the societal divides and empower young people to have access to real options without feeling that one choice they make for a decent living will place them at a disadvantage. Already it is difficult for any young working person to get onto the property ladder. Furthermore, when I visit a school, one of the first questions that I'm asked is whether my job pays well as opposed to questions about the detail of what I do. This implies that they think one job is better than another on the basis of income because, though a job may provide decent work, it will not enable them to live the dream of a decent home. It will lead them and their needs to be treated as second priority - after all, most of the people living in the areas that we classify as socially challenged are decent, hard-working people.

So I go back to the question - what do we want for our children? - Do we really want to compel them to get caught up in the rat race whether they like it or not? Because if we don't do something to begin to address the ever widening gap between the haves and have-nots it will be paramount to taking away their fundamental freedoms of choice

If the standard of education nationally is not what it should be it is time for the adults with responsibility for the curriculum to take responsibility and do something about it now, and time for us to stop criticising the young people who do not actually choose how they are educated. I'm not sure about you but it does nothing to help me if people constantly criticise me and tell me that I'm no good. I think the same applies to young people who are told they education standards are not good enough, although they have worked very hard to meet the standards that have been set for them.

Mind the Gap 2 – Tapping into Diversity

We all live with the objective of being happy;
our lives are all different and yet the same.
Anne Frank

Milton Keynes, as the rest of England, seems to be growing in diversity on a daily basis. If you had come to Milton Keynes 40 years ago, I doubt if you would have come across many black or Asian people as you walked the streets. This is hardly surprising when you consider the rural background of Milton Keynes. Like the rest of England, Milton Keynes has now, however, become very diverse and I personally believe that this is a good thing. Now not only do you see black and Asian people, but people of different origins from all across the world. I believe this makes Milton Keynes all the richer.

As a significant number of people are uncomfortable with both change and the unknown, for a number of the people who lived in Milton Keynes before it became the diverse place it is today the diversity may be disconcerting and uncomfortable. I however believe that our diversity is something to be embraced and learn from. There is such richness to each and every one of us.

If you consider a person as an iceberg, there is the tip that shows above the water which is the little that you can physically see – such as skin colour and gender. Below the water there is so much more to be found such as our values, religious beliefs and beliefs in general, professional and social experiences, language, skills, culture and personality traits. When we take the time to explore what is below water it is often such an exciting experience through which the most amazing things are found. These all entail both similarities and differences that we can all learn from. If you think about the iceberg analogy, the deeper in the sea you are, the wider the variety of fish and other sea creatures.

In 2007, The Hazeley School held a heritage arts exhibition. A number of pupils produced canvas artwork highlighting either their cultures or cultures of their choice. There was a lot of hard work involved in this process, which was put in by pupils and teachers. More importantly I understand that there was a lot of communication and support given through which pupils would have learnt a lot about each other and their cultures. I didn't have much time to speak to the artists, but it was amazing to note how they integrated different cultures into a portrait and the commonalities of portraits representing different cultures.

For the Milton Keynes 40th Birthday Gala, a choir was formed from local Conniborrow residents. The the choir truly represented the diversity of Milton Keynes, certainly in terms of gender, age and colour. I'm sure that there were even deeper levels of diversity within the group than what could be immediately seen. I had the opportunity to speak to a few participants afterwards and found that a number of them had never even met before the choir was formed.

This reiterates the importance that I place on the arts, but it is not just the arts that unite us. There are all sorts of activities within communities that help bridge gaps and foster understanding. We just need to be open to getting involved.

Integration is just as much the responsibility of people coming in (if not more so) as it is of those who are already in residence. I believe there is too much energy concentrated around setting up exclusive groups for people coming in, rather than groups and activities to help them to integrate.

I've heard stories of how some new groups arriving in Milton Keynes have snubbed invitations to join in local community events. I actually find this heartbreaking as, though I believe it is important for people to maintain their unique identity, it is only through integration that we will be able to learn of the richness that dwells beneath the tip of the iceberg.

MIND THE GAPS 3 - EXPECTATIONS

*"The future depends on
what we do in the present.*
MAHATMA GANDHI

As far as I am concerned, it is totally unacceptable for there to be a strong probability that a baby born in one part of the town should automatically be expected to live six years less than babies born in other parts of Milton Keynes, especially if the babies likely to have a shorter lifespan are also from the places with the lowest levels of income, poor health and disability.[17]

It's one thing for some people to live comfortably while others struggle, but when it impacts on people's very existence and becomes a life-or-death situation it becomes totally unacceptable. It may be said that I view things from a moralistic perspective. Maybe I do. I believe a moral standard is crucial when people's lives are at stake.

According to Milton Keynes 2006 Public Health Annual report, the single largest cause of avoidable ill health and premature death is smoking. I guess the seemingly logical response is to say that people should simply stop smoking, start eating healthy food, or stop doing whatever it is that is causing the problems. When you look at things from the perspective of Pandora's Box, it becomes evident that things are not that simple and many issues are often deep-rooted.

I'm not sure if you'll understand this, but I used to smoke, many moons ago when I was in school - I was convinced that it was cool and it helped to relieve stress. Possibly because I was never a heavy smoker - two a day was enough for me - it was quite easy for me to stop and never look back – until recently, while working on this book. I must confess there have been times that some of the things I have heard have distressed me to the extent that I have had an overwhelming urge for a cigarette for some kind of release. At times it has taken everything within me to hold back. Having said all this, the truth remains that the things that have distressed me are not part of my day-to-day existence and, as much as I may empathise, I have a way of escape - my life. With all the issues I may have or face, for me there is always a light at the end of the tunnel and such a way of escape.

I'm not saying stress or pressure is the (only) reason why people smoke; it is a reason and even when it is not, there are other underlying issues that lead people to smoke. Even if smoking is simply a bad habit that an individual actually wants to give up, it's not a priority when there are so many other things going on in an individual's life.

Peter, one of the young people I spoke to, smokes - or hopefully the case is that he used to. When I spoke to him it was his hope that the smoking ban would force him to quit. When he started smoking he was unaware of the implications. For the 12-year-old who asked him for a cigarette, no one had explained the implications to her in a way that she could understand until the day she spoke to Peter.

There is therefore a whole issue or better put – need to educate people on the implications their actions or inactions may have in the case of healthy lifestyles. Beyond education there is also the need to make thing accessible. If not, we will only be dealing with the symptoms and never really bridge the gap.

Bridging the Housing Gap

"The higher we soar,
the smaller we appear to those who cannot fly."
Friedrich Nietzsche

There is a view that a key thing that would make difference to areas with economic deprivation is mixed housing. The probability of houses within existing areas being demolished, making room for mixed housing, is highly unlikely. At the same time, there is likely to be a lot of development around these areas.

Most of the new housing in Central Milton Keynes seems to be unaffordable to the average person. I understand that this is a source of frustration for people who live within the existing areas as it is inaccessible to both them and their families/children. This is especially so for the earlier arrivals to Milton Keynes, who anticipated that housing would be provided to their second generations. They also believe that people within the neighbouring unaffordable housing disassociate from them. (I've been given the example of the relationship between Passmore and Tinkers Bridge).

If new housing within the adjacent areas was more mixed, with much higher proportions of affordable housing within the reach of second-generation families (who would ideally like to live close to their extended families), this would serve as bridging housing, as there would be natural links to the existing areas. Simultaneously, there would be the need to refurbish the existing housing e.g. the rest of the Netherfield roofs.

Mixed housing would need to involve each) developer taking responsibility for both affordable and generally unaffordable housing.

In Medbourne there were five separate developers building housing with unique identities. Four of the developers built unaffordable housing, whilst one built affordable housing. The affordable housing stands out as separate as it is not integrated with the rest of the housing. Subsequently, it is questionable as to whether this is really mixed and in time, this may lead to divides and a separate set of issues.

The expectation is that the development to the neighbouring physical setting and economy would have a knock-on effect on the existing areas and begin to help to deal with the social issues within the existing areas.

Conclusion - Can Do, Will Do?

The reasonable man adapts himself to the world;
the unreasonable one persists in trying to adapt the world to himself.
Therefore all progress depends on the unreasonable man.
George Bernard Shaw Man and Superman (1903) "Maxims for
Revolutionists"
Irish dramatist & socialist (1856 - 1950)

In many ways Milton Keynes is just like any other town across the country. Yet there is something very unique about the place. I've come across very few people who really dislike Milton Keynes. More often than not, those that have something negative to say tend to mock our roundabouts and concrete cows, but I believe this is more due to a lack of understanding than anything else.

The development of the area into a new town was an innovation and a dream built on ideals. Though we have not always got things right, the dreams of Milton Keynes have largely manifested into reality. Possibly this is why Milton Keynes has such a pull for entrepreneurs, innovators and people who believe in dreams – as time and time again the people of Milton Keynes with their can-do attitude have proven that dreams do come true.

As I've said before we do however, have our problems. Many of them are common to the development and growth of an urban area. There are however grave concerns that the newer plans for rapid growth within a very short period of time could cause a new set of avoidable problems if due care, consultation and consideration of all options does not take place. Worse still I hope that we do not over-focus on developing the new at the expense of resolving problems of the old.

I've spent a considerable amount of time talking to people across Milton Keynes and the vast majority of the people that I have spoken to believe in Milton Keynes. Across the city there are people with a knowledge and understanding of the fundamental issues that we have. Many of them have solutions, a number of which are actively being implemented, whilst more support is always appreciated.

Above and beyond everything else I believe there is a need to spend more time listening, hearing and understanding. To get involved in whatever way possible and to work together to continue to develop this town, recognising that we may have differences, but each and every one of us is special with something unique to offer, and that we all, in our different ways, want the best for this town.

The best, however, cannot be the best for a select few but has to be the best for all. We can't afford to leave anyone behind as if we do, if nothing else they will ultimately weigh as down, as we are all more connected than we may realise.

So here is to dynamism, purpose and community from an iconic city that is full of heart and soul and an inviting welcome to visit or even come and abide with us.

In Addition

Some Useful Resources

Benefits Entitlement Calculator – http://www.entitledto.com

Business Networks in Milton Keynes - http://www.tauruspr.co.uk/busnet. htm

Charitable People - http://www.charitablepeople.co.uk/

Citizen's Advice Bureau http://www.citizensadvice.org.uk/

Common Purpose - http://www.commonpurpose.org.uk/

Community Mobilisers - http://www.youtube.com/user/CommunityMobiliser

Connexions Milton Keynes - http://www.connexionsmk.co.uk

Countec - http://www.countec.org/

Credit Union - http://www.mkcreditunion.org.uk/

Discover Milton Keynes Shop: http://www.discovermiltonkeynes.co.uk/

Kik Music - http://www.kikmusic.org.uk/home.html

MKWeb – http://www.mkweb.co.uk

Milton Keynes Chamber of Commerce - http://www.mk-chamber.co.uk/

Milton Keynes Food Bank - http://www.mkfoodbank.org.uk/

Leverage Points – http://www.LeveragePoints.org

Youth Enterprise - http://www.young-enterprise.org.uk/

Price Comparison website - http://www.pricerunner.com

Supermarket Price Comparison website: http://www.mysupermarket.co.uk

Voluntary Sector Websites: http://www.vcsmk.org.uk

Fully up to date list available at www.LeveragePoints.org

Bibliography

Audit Commission (January 2008) "Performance Detailed Report. Partnership and Growth – Phase 2. Milton Keynes Council Audit 2007/08"

Babaee, A. (2007) " Beanhill's Back!" MK News October 10, 2007 pg 3

Bendixson, T. (1992) "Milton Keynes: Image and Reality" Granta Editions

Bletchley & Fenny Stratford Town Council (2007) "Lakes Estate Place Check Results"

Finnegan, R. (1998) "Tales of the City. A Study of Narrative and Urban Life" Cambridge University Press

Clapson, M. (2004) "A Social History of Milton Keynes Middle England/Edge City" Frank Cass Publishers

Clapson,M. Dobbin, M. and Warerman, P (1998) "The Best Laid Plans Milton Keynes since 1967" University of Luton Press

Cook, R. & Shouler, A. (2001) "Milton Keynes in the News" Stroud: Sutton Publishing

Fox, C. (August 2007) "We Must Share in Success" Business MK

Hannam, Laura (January 4, 2008) "Joined-up Thinking on Multi-User Homes" MKNews

Hill, M. Ed. (2007) "The Story of the Original CMK" Living Archive

Hobson, J (1999) "New Towns, The Modernist Planning Project and Social Just. The Cases of Milton Keynes, UK and 6th October, Egypt." Development Planning Unit, University College London

Invest Milton Keynes Facts & Figures 2008

Living Archive Project. "Selected Records" Wolverton, Milton Keynes

MacGregor, S Sunday 22nd April at 11.15am "The Reunion" BBC Radio 4

Milton Keynes Local Strategic Partnership (June 2004) "MK: New Futures. Milton Keynes Community Strategy: Our Handbook for Change 2004-2034)" (Draft for Initial Consultation)

Milton Keynes Census 2001 Data. "Information, Monitoring and Research". Milton Keynes Council

Milton Keynes Community Foundation. "Annual Review 06/07 Inspiring Local Giving for Local Needs"

Milton Keynes Council (2006) "Milton Keynes Social Atlas"

Milton Keynes Council (2006) "Milton Keynes – Responses to Casino Advisory Panel's Supplementary Questions"

Milton Keynes Council/Milton Keynes Primary Care Trust. "Social Atlas for Milton Keynes 2005/2006"

Milton Keynes Development Corporation (1970) "The Plan for Milton Keynes".

Milton Keynes Development Corporation (1971) "Building Conservation in Milton Keynes. A Photographic Index" Martin Cadbury Printing Group

Milton Keynes Development Corporation (1975) "New City Milton Keynes"

Milton Keynes Economy & Learning Partnership (May 2005) "From New Town to International City - the Transformation Years. Strategic Plan 2005-2010"

Milton Keynes Intelligence Observatory: Milton Keynes Borough – Past Population and Projections

Milton Keynes Intelligence Observatory: Age and Highest Qualification by Ethnic group (S117)

Milton Keynes Partnership (July 2006) "The New Plan for Milton Keynes. Growth Strategy to 2031 Sustainability Appraisal."

Milton Keynes Primary Care Trust. "Public Health Annual Report 2006"

Milton Keynes Public Health report 2006

MKNews (2008) "Build More Council Houses Call" MK News January 16 2008 pg 3

NEET Outreach Report. January 2008

Research for Results (2006) "Strategy for Action "Skills and Training Needs Analysis Research Project Summary Report" May 2006

Rib, D. (1980) (ed.) "Write here: Poetry and Short Stories from Writers in Milton Keynes" Milton Keynes: The People's Press

Rok Plc. "Annual Report 2006"

SEEDA. "The Regional Economic Strategy 2006-2016 Implementation Plan"

South East View. "The Regional Perspective. Autumn/Winter 07"

Strategic Urban Futures (March 2008) "Key Principles and Core Elements of the Neighbourhood Regeneration Strategy"

Synnott, M. (December 2007) "A Focal Point for our Accountability" Business MK pg 10

The Concise Oxford Dictionary (Ninth Edition)

The Francis Frith Collection (2005) "So You Think You Know? Milton Keynes. A quiz & Miscellany." Francis Frith Photographic Publishers

The Princes Trust (2007) "The Cost of Exclusion, Counting the cost of youth disadvantage in the UK" The Princes Trust

Urbanis "Exploring the Past, Building the Future in Milton Keynes

Young, M & Willmott, P. (1957) "Family and Kinship in East London". Routledge & Kegan

ENDNOTES

1 Invest Milton Keynes Facts & Figures 2008 Basic Presentation

2 Leverage Points – www.leveragepoints.org

3 Invest Milton Keynes Facts & Figures 2008

4 The Citizen, 3rd April 2008 pg 36

5 MKWeb Religion Section: http://www.mkweb.co.uk/religion/

6 Milton Keynes Intelligence Observatory: Milton Keynes Borough – Past Population and Projections

7 Milton Keynes Intelligence Observatory: Age and Highest Qualification by Ethnic group (S117)

[8] The Cost of Exclusion, Counting the cost of youth disadvantage in the UK. Princes Trust 2007

[9] http://news.bbc.co.uk/1/hi/uk_politics/6506365.stm

[10] http://www.americanidol.com/idolgivesback/

[11] The Concise Oxford Dictionary (Ninth Edition)

[12] Milton Keynes Economic & Learning Partnership website

[13] Schools in Milton Keynes - http://www.schoolswebdirectory.co.uk/leasearch.php?lea=Milton%20Keynes&submit=go

[14] Milton Keynes Social Atlas

[15] Community Mobilisers - http://www.youtube.com/user/CommunityMobiliser

[16] NEET Report, January 2008

[17] Milton Keynes Public Health report 2006, pg 5

Printed in the United Kingdom
by Lightning Source UK Ltd.
135603UK00001B/328-378/P

9 781438 917634